P9-DIY-051

Blended Learning in Higher Education

Blended Learning in Higher Education

Framework, Principles, and Guidelines

D. Randy Garrison

Norman D. Vaughan

JOSSEY-BASS
A Wiley Imprint
www.josseybass.com

Copyright © 2008 by John Wiley & Sons, Inc. All rights reserved.

Published by Jossey-Bass
A Wiley Imprint
989 Market Street, San Francisco, CA 94103-1741—www.josseybass.com

No part of this publication may be reproduced, stored in a retrieval system, or transmitted in any form or by any means, electronic, mechanical, photocopying, recording, scanning, or otherwise, except as permitted under Section 107 or 108 of the 1976 United States Copyright Act, without either the prior written permission of the Publisher, or authorization through payment of the appropriate per-copy fee to the Copyright Clearance Center, Inc., 222 Rosewood Drive, Danvers, MA 01923, 978-750-8400, fax 978-750-4470, or on the web at www.copyright.com. Requests to the Publisher for permission should be addressed to the Permissions Department, John Wiley & Sons, Inc., 111 River Street, Hoboken, NJ 07030, 201-748-6011, fax 201-748-6008, or online at www.wiley.com/go/permissions.

Readers should be aware that Internet Web sites offered as citations and/or sources for further information may have changed or disappeared between the time this was written and when it is read.

Limit of Liability/Disclaimer of Warranty:While the publisher and author have used their best efforts in preparing this book, they make no representations or warranties with respect to the accuracy or completeness of the contents of this book and specifically disclaim any implied warranties of merchantability or fitness for a particular purpose. No warranty may be created or extended by sales representatives or written sales materials. The advice and strategies contained herein may not be suitable for your situation. You should consult with a professional where appropriate. Neither the publisher nor the author shall be liable for any loss of profit or any other commercial damages, including but not limited to special, incidental, consequential, or other damages.

Jossey-Bass books and products are available through most bookstores. To contact Jossey-Bass directly call our Customer Care Department within the U.S. at 800-956-7739, outside the U.S. at 317-572-3986, or fax 317-572-4002.

Jossey-Bass also publishes its books in a variety of electronic formats. Some content that appears in print may not be available in electronic books.

Library of Congress Cataloging-in-Publication Data

Garrison, D. R. (D. Randy), 1945-
  Blended learning in higher education : framework, principles, and guidelines / D. Randy Garrison, Norman D. Vaughan. – 1st ed.
       p. cm.
  Includes bibliographical references and index.
  ISBN 978-0-7879-8770-1 (cloth)
  1. Education, Higher–Computer-assisted instruction. 2. Blended learning. 3. Internet in higher education. I. Vaughan, Norman D., 1960- II. Title.
  LB2395.7.G365 2008
  371.3–dc22

                                                                  2007028790

Printed in the United States of America

FIRST EDITION

HB Printing   10 9 8 7 6 5 4 3 2

The Jossey-Bass Higher and Adult Education Series

Contents

Preface   ix

The Authors   xv

Part One: Community of Inquiry Framework   **1**

1. Introduction   3

2. Community of Inquiry and Blended Learning   13

3. Designing Blended Learning to Create a Community of Inquiry   31

4. Community of Inquiry for Faculty Development   49

Part Two: Blended Learning in Practice   **69**

5. Scenarios   71

6. Guidelines   85

7. Strategies and Tools   105

8. The Future   143

Appendix 1. Organizational Change   157

Appendix 2. Project Proposal Form   173

Appendix 3. Redesign Guide for Blended Learning   177

Appendix 4.   Blended Faculty Community of Inquiry
              Planning Document   181

Appendix 5.   Student Survey Questionnaire   189

Appendix 6.   Faculty Interview Questions   195

Appendix 7.   Student Survey Results   197

Appendix 8.   Faculty Interview Comments   201

Appendix 9.   Template for Preparing a Blended
              Learning Course Outline   205

Appendix 10. Sample Blended Learning Course Outline   207

Appendix 11. Sample Assessment Rubric for an
              e-Portfolio Assignment   219

              References   223

              Index   233

Preface

Higher education institutions must address changing expectations associated with the quality of the learning experience and the wave of technological innovations. Participants in the higher education enterprise are questioning traditional approaches and whether they are achieving the high levels of learning promised. Deep and meaningful learning experiences are best supported by actively engaged learners (Kuh and Associates, 2005). Those who have grown up with interactive technology are not always comfortable with the information transmission approach of large lectures. Students expect a relevant and engaging learning experience.

It is beyond time that higher education institutions recognize the untenable position of holding onto past practices that are incongruent with the needs and demands of a knowledge society. Higher education leaders have the challenge to position their institutions for the twenty-first century. They must provide students with an opportunity to engage their professors and peers in critical and creative reflection and discourse—the conventional ideals of higher education. The past is the future if we examine the ideals of higher education and recognize the need to critically examine current practices in higher education and the potential of communications technology to support intense, varied, and continuous engagement in the learning process. There is the opportunity to revisit and regain the ideals of higher education with the adoption of approaches that value dialogue and debate. The premise of this book is that the greatest possibility of recapturing the ideals of higher education is through redesigning blended learning.

Administration, faculty, and students in higher education know there has to be change in how we design educational experiences. Most recognize that the convergence of the classroom and communications technology has the potential to transform higher education for the better. However, blended learning is more than enhancing lectures. It represents the transformation of how we approach teaching and learning. It is a complete rethinking and redesign of the educational environment and learning experience. Blended learning is a coherent design approach that openly assesses and integrates the strengths of face-to-face and online learning to address worthwhile educational goals. When blended learning is well understood and implemented, higher education will be transformed in a way not seen since the expansion of higher education in the late 1940s. The challenge now is to gain a deep understanding of the need, potential, and strategies of blended learning to approach the ideals of higher education.

The purpose here is to explore the concept of blended learning in a comprehensive yet coherent manner. To borrow from the European ODL Liaison Committee (2004), the challenge is to "create order in the confused 'panacea concept' of 'blended learning' by distinguishing between innovative and merely substitutive use of ICT [information and communication technology]." Several key points are recognized in this statement. The first is the need for order. The second point is the recognition of the complexity of a deceivingly simple concept. And third, blended learning is fundamentally different and is not simply an add-on to the dominant approach. These particular challenges shape the content of this book.

This book provides an organizing framework to guide the exploration and understanding of the principles and practices needed to effect the much needed transformational change in higher education. Moreover, the book provides practical examples and organizational support structures required to fuse a range of face-to-face and online learning to meet the quality challenges and serve disciplinary goals effectively and efficiently.

The primary audience for this book is faculty in higher education who are struggling to find the time and means to engage their students in meaningful learning activities. In addition, faculty who are trying to integrate the Internet and communications technology into their courses will find the book of considerable value. Certainly faculty developers and instructional designers will find here a coherent approach and specific techniques for designing blended learning courses. Finally, graduate students and administrators will find this book useful to gain an understanding and appreciation for the potential of blended learning designs.

Overview of Contents

Blended Learning in Higher Education provides a vision and a roadmap for higher education faculty to understand the possibilities of organically blending face-to-face and online learning for engaging and meaningful learning experiences. The first part provides the theoretical framework. The second part focuses on the practice of designing a blended learning experience.

Chapter One explores the broader context that has spawned the interest in and development of blended learning in higher education. The chapter describes blended learning, along with changing expectations and challenges in higher education. It then discusses how blended learning can address these challenges through its potential to merge the best of face-to-face and online approaches.

Part One: Community of Inquiry Framework

Chapter Two introduces the community of inquiry framework as the ideal and heart of a higher education experience. The framework provides the roadmap for the integration of face-to-face and online learning activities. The chapter describes the conceptual foundation in terms of purposeful, open, and disciplined critical discourse and reflection. It also discusses the core elements of the framework—social, cognitive, and teaching presence.

Chapter Three outlines seven blended learning redesign principles. The chapter spans the three categories of teaching presence—design, facilitation, and direct instruction—and describes and identifies the principles of social and cognitive presence in each of these categories, as well as assessment.

Chapter Four uses the community of inquiry framework to explore professional development issues essential to the implementation of blended learning designs. It also describes faculty learning communities, organizational strategies for support, and blended approaches to professional development.

Part Two: Blended Learning in Practice

Chapter Five presents six scenarios of blended learning design organized under three ideal types. Each of the scenarios reflects successful blended learning designs associated with courses common in higher education. They cut across disciplines and are an amalgam of the best features and examples of course redesigns based upon the authors' experiences and those found in the literature. They serve as the touchstone for further discussions in designing blended approaches to learning in higher education.

Chapter Six explores more practical guidelines to blended learning redesign. It begins with a discussion of new approaches congruent with higher education goals. The discussion then moves into specific guidelines with regard to applying the previously identified principles.

Chapter Seven describes specific techniques and tools to engage students in a collaborative and reflective blended learning experience. It gives detailed examples such as an online syllabus, a lesson plan for the first week, discussion forums, assessment rubrics, and other practical ideas and tips. These techniques and tools can be readily adapted to a range of disciplinary contexts.

Chapter Eight describes the era of engagement and looks into the near future with a discussion of the evolutionary transformation of teaching and learning in higher education. Finally, the Appendixes provide a wide range of documents, practical tools, and resources.

Although chapters may be read in any order, the chapters do build on particular themes and concepts, and in many cases they follow a similar structure. For this reason, the most benefit from the book can be gained by reading the chapters in sequence.

Acknowledgments

We would like to recognize the blended learning resources that B. J. Eib, Patti Dyjur, Julie Weible, and Rosalie Pedersen have developed at the University of Calgary, which we have incorporated into this book. In addition, we would like to thank the University of Calgary professors who shared with us their experiences and insights in designing blended learning courses. We would be remiss not to acknowledge and thank David Brightman at Jossey-Bass for his insightful suggestions to improve the first draft of the manuscript.

We would also like to acknowledge that Chapter Three grew out of a previously published article: Garrison, D. R. (2006). Online collaboration principles. *Journal of Asynchronous Learning Networks*, 10(1), 25–34.

The Authors

D. Randy Garrison is the director of the Teaching & Learning Centre and a full professor in the Faculty of Education at the University of Calgary. He served as dean, faculty of extension at the University of Alberta from 1996 to 2001. He has published extensively on teaching and learning in higher, distance, and adult education contexts. This is his sixth book, and he has published well in excess of 100 refereed articles. Randy Garrison has won several research awards.

Norman D. Vaughan is the coordinator for the inquiry and blended learning program in the Teaching & Learning Centre at the University of Calgary. In this position he coordinates course redesign projects and provides support for the faculty and graduate student teaching certificate programs. Norm is also a member of the editorial boards for the *Journal on Excellence in College Teaching* and the *Canadian Journal of Learning and Technology*. His teaching background includes graduate and undergraduate courses in educational technology, K–12 education in northern Canada, technical training in the petroleum industry, and English as a second language in Japan. In addition, he has been involved in several consulting projects with book publishers and higher education institutions to develop online courses and resources. Norm received his Ph.D. in Educational Technology from the University of Calgary. His current research focuses on blended learning and faculty development.

Blended Learning in Higher Education

Part One

COMMUNITY OF INQUIRY FRAMEWORK

1

INTRODUCTION

In this chapter we document the growing interest in blended learning and describe the essence of this emerging approach to course design. We also make the case for a framework that has practical value in guiding blended learning design and describe the challenges in understanding and implementing this potentially significant change in higher education. We encourage educators in higher education to reexamine current practices and to actively engage students in their learning to achieve the higher-order learning outcomes that are so needed in higher education (Boyer Commission, 2001). New ways of thinking about course design are required to reconcile traditional values and practices with evolving expectations and technological possibilities.

Interest in Blended Learning

Curtis Bonk and his colleagues have documented the strong and growing interest in blended learning (Bonk & Graham, 2006). They concluded in a recent survey of higher education that respondents clearly expected a dramatic rise in their use of blended learning approaches in the coming years (Bonk, Kim & Zeng, 2006, p. 553). In another survey, Arabasz and Baker (2003) revealed that 80 percent of all higher education institutions offer blended learning courses.

Underlying these data is the increasing awareness that blended learning approaches and designs can significantly enhance the learning experience. Albrecht (2006) reports high student satisfaction with blended learning, and others have reported faculty satisfaction (Vaughan & Garrison, 2006a). This is confirmed by Marquis (2004) in a survey that found that 94 percent of lecturers believed that blended learning "is more effective than classroom-based teaching alone." This is also consistent with a study by Bourne and Seaman (2005), who found that the primary interest in blended learning is to benefit the educational process. They report that blended learning is perceived to be a means to combine the best of face-to-face and online learning.

The need to provide more engaged learning experiences is at the core of the interest in blended learning. Many faculty have begun to question passive teaching and learning approaches such as the lecture. The lecture is a method of disseminating information that emerged before the advent of the printing press. The lecture is not particularly effective in engaging learners in critically filtering and making sense of the glut of information that we now face. Complex topics require more in-depth engagement for students to construct meaning than what is possible in a typical lecture. In this regard, Palloff and Pratt (2005) argue that interactive and collaborative learning experiences are more congruent with achieving higher-order learning outcomes.

Concurrent with the recognition of the importance of interactive and engaged learning experiences is the growing understanding of the potential of the Internet and communications technology to connect learners. The interest in blended learning can also be attributed to the advances and proliferation of communications technology in most segments of society—advances that have not seen the same degree of uptake in the higher education classroom. Although this is changing, there is still a lack of understanding of how best to use technology to advance the goals of higher education in terms of engaging students in critical thinking and discourse.

We argue that the time has come to reject the dualistic thinking that seems to demand choosing between conventional face-to-face and online learning, a dualism that is no longer tenable, theoretically or practically. There is a better approach. With the increasing awareness and adoption of the Internet and communications technology to connect learners, a more sensible way forward would be to better understand the potential of these technologies and how they might be integrated with the best of the face-to-face learning environment.

We explore in this book a new educational paradigm that integrates the strengths of face-to-face and online learning. Blended learning—a design approach whereby both face-to-face and online learning are made better by the presence of the other—offers the possibility of recapturing the traditional values of higher education while meeting the demands and needs of the twenty-first century.

Blended Learning Described

Recognizing true blended learning is not obvious. Blended learning is the thoughtful fusion of face-to-face and online learning experiences. The basic principle is that face-to-face oral communication and online written communication are optimally integrated such that the strengths of each are blended into a unique learning experience congruent with the context and intended educational purpose. Although the concept of blended learning may be intuitively apparent and simple, the practical application is more complex. Blended learning is not an addition that simply builds another expensive educational layer. It represents a restructuring of class contact hours with the goal to enhance engagement and to extend access to Internet-based learning opportunities. Most important, blended learning is a fundamental redesign that transforms the structure of, and approach to, teaching and learning. The key assumptions of a blended learning design are

- Thoughtfully integrating face-to-face and online learning
- Fundamentally rethinking the course design to optimize student engagement
- Restructuring and replacing traditional class contact hours

Blended learning emerges from an understanding of the relative strengths of face-to-face and online learning. This opens a wide range of possibilities for redesign that goes beyond enhancing the traditional classroom lecture. Attaining the threshold of blended learning means replacing aspects of face-to-face learning with appropriate online learning experiences, such as labs, simulations, tutorials, and assessment. Blended learning represents a new approach and mix of classroom and online activities consistent with the goals of specific courses or programs.

Blended learning must be approached with the awareness of the broad range of flexible design possibilities and the challenge of doing things differently. It must be based upon a sound understanding of higher-order learning environments, communication characteristics, requirements of various disciplines, and resources. Blended learning redesign is a catalyst; it means to fundamentally reconceptualize and restructure the teaching and learning transaction. Its basic assumption is to open the educational mind to a full range of possibilities. Blended learning brings into consideration a range of options that require revisiting how students learn in deep and meaningful ways.

Blended learning is no more about reshaping and enhancing the traditional classroom than it is about making e-learning more acceptable. In both contexts one is left with essentially either face-to-face or online learning. Blended learning combines the properties and possibilities of both to go beyond the capabilities of each separately. It recognizes the strengths of integrating verbal and text-based communication and creates a unique fusion of synchronous and asynchronous, direct and mediated modes of communication in that the proportion of face-to-face and online learning activities may vary considerably.

Blended learning necessitates that educators question what is important and consider how much time should be spent in the classroom. We approach the possibilities of blended learning only when we step back and allow our minds to escape the paradigmatic trap of either the traditional lecture or Web-based learning. Blended learning is an approach to educational redesign that can enhance and extend learning and offer designs that efficiently manage large classes. It represents a distinct design methodology that transcends the conventional classroom paradigm. The proportion of face-to-face and online learning activities may vary considerably, but blended learning is distinguishable by way of the integration of face-to-face and online learning that is multiplicative, not additive.

Change

Higher education must start delivering on its promise of providing learning experiences that engage and address the needs of society in the twenty-first century. As Swail (2002) states, the "rules are changing, and there is increased pressure on institutions of higher education to evolve, adapt, or desist" (p. 16). To paraphrase Peter Drucker (1999), we must ask ourselves: would we, knowing what we now know, design learning experiences as we do with 200 and 300 students in a lecture hall? With what we know about the potential of blended learning, the need to create communities of inquiry, and the vast array of accessible and affordable communications technology, the answer has to be that there must be a better way.

Levy (2005) has stated that the field of e-learning "is marked by a juxtaposition of new technology and old pedagogy." Higher education is only just beginning to grasp the significance and educational potential of asynchronous communication networks. The mistake of most traditional campus-based institutions was to see the potential of online learning in terms of access and serving more students instead of serving current students better. However, serving students *better* from a learning perspective would necessitate the adoption of a new pedagogy. For the traditional campus-based higher education institution, the breakthrough came when online learning was no longer regarded as a substitute but as an integral and valued component to address the need for a new pedagogy. This was the watershed moment for higher education.

The transformation of teaching and learning in higher education is inevitable with the use of Web-based communications technology (Newman, Couturier & Scurry, 2004). Fundamental redesign based on blended approaches to teaching and learning represent the means to address the challenges associated with providing a quality learning experience. Although the catalyst for change in teaching and learning has been technology, it is the need to enhance quality standards that is drawing attention to the potential of blended approaches. Technology is an enabling tool. Because blended learning is an approach and design that merges the best of traditional and Web-based learning experiences to create and sustain vital communities of inquiry, many higher education institutions are quietly positioning themselves to harness its transformational potential.

The Framework

Blended learning is at the center of an evolutionary transformation of teaching and learning in higher education. However, transformational growth can only be sustained with a clear understanding of the nature of the educational process and intended learning outcomes. In higher education there is an expressed focus on opportunities for learners to construct meaning and confirm understanding through discourse. At the core of this process is a community of inquiry that supports connection and collaboration among learners and creates a learning environment that integrates social, cognitive, and teaching elements in a way that will precipitate and sustain critical reflection and discourse. Blended learning opens the possibility of creating and sustaining a community of inquiry beyond the classroom.

We approach the understanding of blended learning designs through the framework of a community of inquiry. The community of inquiry (CoI) framework was created by Garrison and his colleagues (2000) to guide the research and practice of online learning. The CoI framework was generated from the literature and experiences of the authors grounded in the larger field of education. In particular, the framework was grounded in a critical, collaborative learning community consistent with the ideals of higher education. The generic nature of the framework and its resonance with both face-to-face and online education make it a useful guide to understand and design blended learning environments.

Arbaugh (2006) states that the CoI framework has shown considerable promise and has been widely cited in the literature. One reason for this is that it is a comprehensive yet parsimonious and intuitively understandable framework. Another reason is that it builds upon two ideas that are essential to higher education—*community* and *inquiry*. Community, on the one hand, recognizes the social nature of education and the role that interaction, collaboration, and discourse play in constructing knowledge. Inquiry, on the other hand, reflects the process of constructing meaning through personal responsibility and choice. A community of inquiry is a cohesive and interactive community of learners whose purpose is to critically analyze, construct, and confirm worthwhile knowledge. The three key elements for a viable community of inquiry are social presence, teaching presence, and cognitive presence. A community of inquiry appropriately integrates these elements and provides a means to guide the design of deep and meaningful educational experiences.

We use the CoI framework to shape this book. The first part of the book focuses on understanding this perspective and describing how it can influence practice and professional development. The design scenarios, guidelines, strategies, and tools discussed in the second part of this book all emerge from the CoI framework. The next chapter describes the CoI framework in greater detail.

Conclusion

There has been little fundamental change with regard to how we approach teaching and learning in higher education, yet there is increasing dissatisfaction among faculty, students, and society with the quality of the learning experience. Although technological advancements in society have been unrelenting (the Internet, pocket-sized computers, wireless web, cell phones, and satellite radio, television, games, and simulations), technological innovation in higher education has been largely restricted to administration and research. The significant technological innovations in teaching and learning have been confined to addressing issues of access and convenience. However, addressing the relevance and quality of the learning experience demands that higher education take a fresh look at how it approaches teaching and learning and utilizes technology.

For all of these reasons, as well as because of the successes of individual blended learning designs, there is a convergence of interest (intuitive appeal), need (educational demands) and opportunity (potential of communications technology) with regard to blended learning. The reality of engaging students across time and place makes possible the educational ideal of an engaged community of inquiry. Blended learning designs remove the constraints to create and sustain communities of inquiry in higher education.

The concept of a community of inquiry that frames this book provides a much needed roadmap for blended learning approaches and designs. The CoI framework provides the order and rationality to understand the nature, purpose, and principles of blended learning. It provides the context for the practical examples and the selection of strategies and tools presented in this book. It also generates the rationale for the templates and rubrics found in the Appendix.

Blended learning is not new. What is new is the recognition of its potential to help fundamentally redesign the learning experience in ways that can enhance the traditional values of higher education. Blended learning can address the ideals and core values of higher education in terms of creating and sustaining communities of inquiry. The challenge higher education faces is how to merge the distinct approaches and properties of face-to-face and online learning. This challenge is the focus of the remaining chapters of this book.

2

COMMUNITY OF INQUIRY AND BLENDED LEARNING

The rationale and guidelines for blended learning provided here are embedded within the community of inquiry (CoI) framework. A framework avoids the distortion that may arise from the separation of theory and practice. Without order and a means to construct the rationale for adopting a particular technique, we are condemned to thrash about and to randomly search for what may work with little understanding of why something was successful or not. A coherent framework avoids the tyranny of adopting clever techniques. Moreover, a theoretical framework not only provides a means to shape practice but also to reflect upon and make sense of outcomes. The openness of blended learning redesigns, in terms of the range of possibilities, demands a strong theoretical foundation and framework.

A blended learning framework must organically integrate thought and action and provide an understanding for the importance of sustained critical discourse and private reflection. A unified framework will merge the public and private worlds. Finally, a useful blended learning framework must be coherent and inform the integration of face-to-face and online learning.

Conceptual Foundation

In recent years, innovative approaches to teaching and learning in higher education were inevitably framed from a constructivist perspective. Constructivist learning theory is essentially about individuals making sense of their experiences. However, meaning

13

is not constructed in isolation. Consistent with Garrison and Archer (2000), we believe the ideal educational transaction is a collaborative constructivist process that has inquiry at its core. Social interaction and collaboration shapes and tests meaning, thus enriching understanding and knowledge sharing. It is important to note that collaborative constructivist learning experiences are not conducive to "covering" a large amount of subject matter. Instead, the emphasis is on inquiry processes that ensure core concepts are constructed and assimilated in a deep and meaningful manner.

The theoretical foundation for blended learning as outlined here is predicated on the recognition of the unity of the public and private worlds, information and knowledge, discourse and reflection, control and responsibility, and process with learning outcomes. John Dewey strongly rejected dualism and argued that the value of the educative experience is in unifying the internal and external worlds. Dewey stated, "the educational process has two sides—one psychological and one sociological; and that neither can be subordinated to the other or neglected without evil results following" (1959, p. 20). It is essential that students be actively engaged in the process of inquiry. When action is divorced from thought, teaching becomes information "transmission by a kind of scholastic pipeline into the minds of pupils whose business is to absorb what is transmitted" (Dewey & Childs, 1981, pp. 88–89). For this reason, higher education experiences are best conceived as communities of inquiry.

A community of inquiry is inevitably described as the ideal and heart of a higher education experience. A community of inquiry is shaped by purposeful, open, and disciplined critical discourse and reflection.

Purposeful

According to Dewey, educational inquiry is a process to investigate problems and issues—not to memorize solutions. Inquiry within the educational community focuses on intended goals and learning outcomes. It is a systematic process to define relevant questions, search for relevant information, formulate solutions, and apply those solutions. Discourse engages curriculum through reflection. A community of inquiry depends on sustained communication and collaboration wherein participants share experience and insights. Participants are expected to be self-directed and focused on the task at hand.

Education defined as a process of inquiry goes beyond accessing or even assimilating information. Inquiry joins process and outcomes (means-end) in a unified, iterative cycle. It links reflection and content by encouraging students to collaboratively explore and reasonably question the organization and meaning of subject matter. Inquiry is both a reflective and collaborative experience. Inquiry must be purposeful, but flexible, to explore unintended paths of interest. Personal relationships may be an artifact of a successful community of inquiry, but they are not the primary goal. Sustained communities of inquiry are dependent upon purposeful and respectful relations that encourage free and open communication.

Open

The individual must have the freedom to explore ideas, question, and construct meaning. If learning is to be a process of inquiry, then it must focus on questions, not just on answers. Learners must be free to follow new leads and to question public knowledge. They must have an opportunity to explore questions, as well as to construct and confirm resolutions collaboratively. Paavola and colleagues argue that constructing individual meaning and "knowledge creation is a matter of individual initiative embedded in fertile group . . . activities" (Paavola, Lipponen, & Hakkarainen, 2004, p. 568). Schrire (2004) found a relationship between interaction and cognition. We believe that understanding is precipitated and enhanced through interaction in the community. Education does not easily advance to higher levels of inquiry when reflection and discourse are artificially severed.

The inquiry method is dependent upon interaction. Interaction is essential for both a community of inquiry and the higher educational experience. The educational process within this community is a process of inquiry that integrates both the public and private worlds. Participants must feel secure to reveal their private thoughts and open them to scrutiny and critique. Engagement in a community of inquiry is the intersection of public and private worlds. An educational experience has both an interactive (social) and a reflective (private) element. To inquire is to be awakened, informed, and engaged to explore the controversies of a discipline rather than simply adopt the obvious and accepted truths. Worthwhile educational experiences fully engage learners to question ideas—even accepted truths—and hone the critical and creative thinking abilities of students.

Disciplined

The foreground of the educational experience is engagement—interaction, collaboration, and reflection. The educational experience requires focusing on ideas and conceptual frameworks, challenging and creating ideas, and diagnosing misconceptions and constructing mutual understanding. It demands the discipline to interact academically and respectfully with members of the community as they engage in the pursuit of common goals. It is learning to listen, explain, and defend positions and ideas. In short, the educational experience is a commitment to scholarship. By focusing on the process of inquiry, higher-order thinking and learning emerge. Lipman (1991) defined higher-order thinking as being "conceptually rich, coherently organized, and persistently exploratory" (p. 19). The process of inquiry requires considerable intellectual discipline. In a discipline of inquiry, participants acquire the attitudes and skills to become critical thinkers and to continue their learning beyond the narrow scope and time limit of a formal educational experience.

Discipline is essential for deep and meaningful learning. Discipline provides the mindset to engage in critical discourse and reflection. For tacit knowledge and individual insights to be externalized and made explicit, participants must have the discipline to engage in critical reflection and discourse. A community of inquiry requires discipline if it is to provide a sense of connection and support in the systematic and purposeful pursuit of shared educational goals and knowledge. Through purposeful, open, and disciplined interaction and discourse, a community supports inquiry and development of both the individual and the community. Disciplined collaboration to test and confirm personally constructed meaning is essential and integral to a community of inquiry.

The following CoI framework provides a broad orientation to the educational process. This framework will provide order and guide our exploration of blended learning designs by presenting a coherent and accurate account of what shapes educational processes and outcomes.

Community of Inquiry

An educational community is a formally constituted group of individuals whose connection is that of academic purpose and interest who work collaboratively toward intended learning goals and outcomes. The purpose of the community should determine how it is defined and developed. From an educational perspective, the academic interest should be the primary focus. Community must be developed to support the learning processes that progress systematically from identifying a problem to resolving it. Participant knowledge and expertise is shared and developed through discourse and collaborative activities. Although social dynamics are important to create the climate that will support the learning process, it is the academic interests that give purpose and shape to the inquiry process. Roles and expectations are defined by the educational community.

As noted, the CoI framework provides much of the conceptual order for this book and has shown strong empirical validation (Arbaugh, 2007; Garrison, Cleveland-Innes, & Fung, 2004). The community of inquiry is a recursive model in that each of the core elements supports the others (see Figure 2.1). The three elements of the CoI framework are social presence, cognitive presence, and teaching presence. Each of the presences reflects categories and indicators that operationalize the elements used to study and design the teaching and learning transaction. It is important to

Figure 2.1 Community of Inquiry Framework

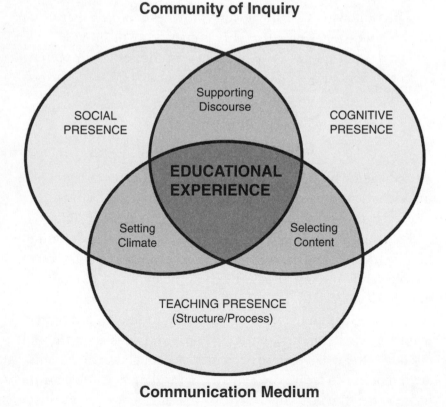

Community of Inquiry

SOCIAL PRESENCE

Supporting Discourse

COGNITIVE PRESENCE

EDUCATIONAL EXPERIENCE

Setting Climate

Selecting Content

TEACHING PRESENCE
(Structure/Process)

Communication Medium

note the interdependence across and within the presences. For example, teaching presence will have a significant influence on cognitive presence, and social presence will influence cognitive presence. Overlap does not have to be symmetrical. Emphasis can be on any one of the presences.

We next describe the presences crucial for the design of a blended educational experience.

Social Presence

Students in a community of inquiry must feel free to express themselves openly in a risk-free manner. They must be able to develop the personal relationships necessary to commit to, and pursue, intended academic goals and gain a sense of belonging to the community. The formal categories of social presence are open communication, cohesive responses, and affective/personal connections (see Table 2.1). These categories are progressive in the sense that they establish, sustain, and develop a community of inquiry.

Meaningful communication begins when students can communicate openly. Community is established when students are

Table 2.1 Community of Inquiry Categories and Indicators

Elements	Categories	Indicators (examples only)
Social presence	Open communication Group cohesion Affective/personal	Enabling risk-free expression Encouraging collaboration Expressing emotions, camaraderie
Cognitive presence	Triggering event Exploration Integration Resolution	Having sense of puzzlement Exchanging information Connecting ideas Applying new ideas
Teaching presence	Design & organization Facilitation of discourse Direct instruction	Setting curriculum and methods Sharing personal meaning Focusing discussion

encouraged to project themselves personally and academically. Interpersonal interaction is a very important means of connecting with others and creating trust. A community of inquiry must foster personal but purposeful relationships. Students must feel emotionally secure to engage in open, purposeful discourse. Students may well feel secure and feel free to comment but may still need to establish the cohesiveness for the community to begin to work collaboratively. A community is inherently collaborative. Therefore, social presence must provide the cohesive tension to sustain participation and focus. Although participants must be respected as individuals, they must also feel a sense of responsibility and commitment to the community of inquiry. Open communication establishes a community of inquiry, but social cohesion sustains it. Finally, according to Ruth Brown (2001), "after long-term and/or intense association with others involving personal communication" (p. 24), personal relationships develop and camaraderie may emerge. In a community of inquiry, it takes time for students to find a level of comfort and trust, develop personal relationships, and evolve into a state of camaraderie. Emotional bonding and camaraderie constitute the ultimate stage of establishing social presence in an educational community.

Considerable research has focused on the issue of social presence in computer conferencing. There was great concern in the early research that the lack of visual cues and body language would seriously inhibit the effectiveness of asynchronous text communication. Put simply, the communication theorists argued that the lack of social cues would severely limit interpersonal communication. However, researchers began to understand the complexities of this supposedly "lean" communication medium. It became clear that participants could communicate a wide range of socio-emotional messages, such as personal greetings, feelings, and humor. Written communication, in fact, had great power and flexibility and participants could project themselves socially and emotionally and create interpersonal relationships.

Establishing social presence is a primary concern at the outset of creating a community of inquiry. Social relationships create a sense of belonging, support freedom of expression, and sustain cohesiveness, but they do not structure and focus academic interests among the students. Social interaction is insufficient to sustain a community of inquiry and achieve educational goals. Communities of inquiry are more than online chat rooms. Higher levels of learning inevitably require purposeful discourse to collaboratively construct, critically reflect, and confirm understanding. This is what is referred to as cognitive presence. With the understanding that social presence could be established in a community of inquiry, we next turn our attention to issues of cognitive and teaching presence.

Cognitive Presence

Cognitive presence is basic to the inquiry process. Inquiry includes the integration of reflective and interactive processes. Cognitive presence maps the cyclical inquiry pattern of learning from experience through reflection and conceptualization to action and on to further experience (see Figure 2.2). We see the progressive nature of cognitive presence moving from a triggering event through to resolution. Dewey based his concept of inquiry on the scientific process writ large. This is the core of cognitive presence and a key element of the CoI framework.

Cognitive presence is defined by the practical inquiry model (see Figure 2.2). In comparison to other cognitive taxonomies, Schrire (2004) found the practical inquiry model "to be the most relevant to the analysis of the cognitive dimension and presents a clear picture of the knowledge-building processes" (p. 491). Practical inquiry has two dimensions and four phases. The vertical axis defines the deliberation–action dimension. This dimension represents the recursive nature of inquiry as representing both constructive and collaborative activities. The horizontal axis represents the perception–conception dimension. This process

Figure 2.2 Practical Inquiry Model

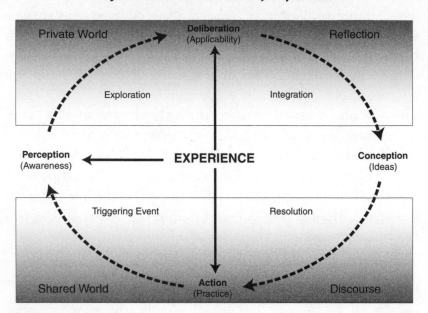

constructs meaning from experience. Although the dimensions are abstracted processes, the phases of inquiry resemble more closely the educational experience. The first phase is the triggering event, whereby an issue or problem is identified and defined. The second phase is the exploration of the problem and the gathering and refinement of relevant information. In the third phase, participants begin to reconcile and make sense of the information. Solutions will be hypothesized and debated. In the final phase, the preferred solution is applied and tested directly or vicariously. It may trigger another cycle of inquiry if the solution is not satisfactory.

Cognitive presence is a recursive process that encompasses states of puzzlement, information exchange, connection of ideas, creation of concepts, and the testing of the viability of solutions. This is not to suggest, however, that the actual practice of inquiry is linear or immutable. Some problems or issues will be more inductive and will require students to focus more on exploration. Others will be more deductive and students will focus on the application of ideas or solutions. Leaps of insight and intuition reflect what appears to be radical phase shifts such as a student moving from exploration spontaneously to a solution. Regardless, practical inquiry must be a logical process and hypothesized solutions rationally justified and defended. A community of inquiry is essential to establish and sustain cognitive presence.

Higher educational outcomes are very difficult to define and measure. Moreover, outcomes change as students engage in the educational process and activities are modified. As Burbules (2004) states, "Outcomes are constituted and reconstituted in active processes of inquiry, not taken as static endpoints" (p. 7). Unfortunately, an obsession with educational outcomes has created a focus on assimilating measurable, although trivial, information. Unintended learning outcomes can be most educational. True inquiry is exploratory and often unpredictable. Burbules (2004) goes on to say that the "question of educational quality should be sought . . . in the reflexively critical and liberating activities of the classroom itself" (p. 9). For this reason, practical inquiry is very much process oriented.

Establishing and maintaining cognitive presence in blended communities is the area that is in greatest need of research. Cognitive presence goes to the heart of a community of interest. It has been argued that community supports the cognitive development of individuals. Garrison and Archer (2007) point out that only recently has research focused on the nature of formal, purposive online educational communities and their ability to support cognitive presence. Heckman and Annabi (2005) found written communication to be cognitively rich. Not only was written communication precise and permanent, but it was open to all participants in a way not always possible in a face-to-face context. Working in an asynchronous text-based environment reduces student cognitive load and the need to rely on memory to process large numbers of facts and ideas. Cognition and learning, above a very limited number of facts and ideas, is inversely proportional to the cognitive load. Online inquiry would appear to offer students a considerable advantage in processing information and constructing meaning.

Online communities of inquiry were also shown to be more inclusive and less threatening. Other researchers have shown that a sense of community is positively related to the perception of learning in an online environment (Rovai, 2002; Shea et al., 2006). However, little cognitive presence research has focused on blended learning environments and the strengths of integrating verbal and written communication.

The final element necessary to create and sustain a community of inquiry is teaching presence. Teaching presence is essential to provide structure, facilitation, and direction for the cohesion, balance, and progression of the inquiry process.

Teaching Presence

In an educational context, teaching presence is essential to bring all the elements together and ensure that the community of interest is productive. It is a significant educational challenge to create and sustain a community of inquiry. Teaching presence provides the design, facilitation, and direction for a worthwhile educational experience (see Figure 2.2). There is evidence of construct validity for teaching presence (Arbaugh, 2007; LaPointe & Gunawardena, 2004). Consistent with the categories of social and cognitive presence, these are progressive; they do not reflect static categories. Although the categories are always present (for example, planning occurs throughout the educational process), the different categories take precedence as the inquiry process moves from planning to establishing and sustaining reflection and discourse. Teaching presence establishes the curriculum, approaches, and methods; it also moderates, guides, and focuses discourse and tasks. It is the means by which to bring together social and cognitive presence in an effective and efficient manner. Teaching presence is an essential and challenging responsibility, especially in a blended learning environment where students are not always in direct contact.

The focus of recent research has shifted to teaching presence. In a review of the CoI literature, Garrison (2006b) has shown that students in an online CoI expect strong teaching presence. Perry and Edwards (2005) state that "exemplary online teachers create a community of inquiry that is comprised of a strong social, cognitive and teaching presence." From an online teaching-effectiveness perspective, Conrad (2005) reports in her research that students stated simply that "Good instructors created community; poor instructors didn't" (p. 12). She also states that opportunity for face-to-face experiences can enhance connectedness and satisfaction. Similarly, Garrison and Cleveland-Innes, (2005) found that students value their time and expect structure and leadership. Arbaugh (2007) found teaching presence to be a strong predictor of perceived learning and satisfaction with the delivery medium. Finally, Dixson and associates (2006) found that leadership was linked to student success. Students clearly attribute a successful learning experience with teaching presence. The unifying force of teaching presence is essential to create and sustain a community of inquiry in a blended environment when students are shifting between direct and mediated communication.

Blended learning is about fully engaging students in the educational process; that is, providing students with a highly interactive succession of learning experiences that lead to the resolution of an issue or problem. Interaction is to life in the classroom what carbon is to DNA. However, just as other elements (hydrogen, oxygen, and nitrogen) are essential to the formation of DNA, cognitive and social presence in the classroom also require the components of design, facilitation, and direction to form a vital community of inquiry that will ensure organic academic growth and development.

The provision of teaching presence is challenged to shape cognitive and metacognitive processes and learning. Student awareness of the inquiry process is crucial to complete the inquiry cycle and to prevent stalling in the early phases. Metacognitive awareness must be a goal of higher education for students to monitor and manage their learning. Metacognition is the regulation of cognition, which includes self-appraisal (assessing what needs to be done) and self-management (successfully carrying out the learning task). Engaging in a higher-order learning experience requires that students have some metacognitive understanding of the inquiry process if students are to learn how to learn.

The CoI framework provides an understanding of the essential elements of a higher educational experience. The goal is to use this framework to explore the synergies of face-to-face and online learning.

Real and Virtual Communities

Blended learning is a significant presence in higher education that offers contact and convenience for the professor and students. The strength of blended learning goes beyond the complementary educational experiences of face-to-face and online learning. Blended learning represents a fundamental redesign and the consideration of new approaches to learning. The premise is that education is best experienced in a community of inquiry. How we integrate real and virtual communities will be informed by the community of inquiry model and related research.

Dewey (1981) believed in the "experience of genuine community" and continuous inquiry "in the sense of being connected as well as persistent" (p. 620). Being connected and persistent gives participants the means to shape the discourse and be fully engaged. Empirically, Rovai and Jordan (2004) found that "blended courses produce a stronger sense of community among students than either traditional or fully online courses." In turn, Rovai (2002) and others have found that community is associated with higher levels of perceived learning (Schrire, 2004; Shea et al., 2006).

Community is not defined by physical presence. Network supported and facilitated communities have the great advantage of being accessible virtually anywhere and at any time. Shumar and Renninger (2002) argue that online or virtual communities can be simultaneously expanded and compressed in space and time. Although it may be clear how communities can be sustained over time, the written form of communication can also compress time with succinct and more rapid forms of communication compared to spontaneous and ephemeral verbal exchanges. Face-to-face verbal and online text communication are distinct and have enormous potential to complement each other. Conrad (2005) found that when online learners had an opportunity to meet face-to-face, they reported "an enormous surge in connectedness and satisfaction with the program design" (p. 9). She also reported that face-to-face and online communication "facilitated a greater ease in the other medium" (p. 9). Reciprocity benefited teacher-student and student-student relationships and learning in both face-to-face and online environments.

Blended learning has enormous potential to transform the nature of the educational experience with the use of direct and mediated communication and the rethinking of the educational approach. Shumar and Renninger (2002) state that the "boundary between the physical and virtual communities is permeable, . . . making it difficult to conceptualize either form of community as a completely separate entity" (p. 8). The community of participants may be well defined, but the network is virtually infinite. Blended learning is a complex weaving of the face-to-face and online communities so that participants move between them in a seamless manner—each with its complementary strengths. Communication in such a community is multidimensional, both academically and personally. Blended learning communities open up new learning relationships that can extend beyond the limited time of the class and course.

It is a challenge to create and sustain an online community of inquiry. An educational community is a specialized and purposeful community that must come together quickly but lasts for a relatively short period. Fully online communities take time to develop social and cognitive presence to support the necessary commitment and collaboration. Face-to-face communication provides an opportunity to create a sense of community and connectedness more quickly. Although a face-to-face classroom dynamic may provide the best opportunity to begin the formation of a community, online communities can extend the opportunity for both sustained and flexible communication and provide convenient links to other resources.

However, other personal and collaborative properties and capacities of face-to-face and online learning need to be considered. Garrison and colleagues have shown that "students do perceive face-to-face and online learning differently" (Garrison, Cleveland-Innes, & Fung, 2004, p. 70). Furthermore, they suggest that the face-to-face learning experience is more teacher oriented, whereas the online learning experience is more cognitive or internally focused. They also observe that the face-to-face educational experience involves the teacher transmitting information, in "contrast to online learning which is concurrent with and integral to the learning process" (p. 70).

How we integrate face-to-face and online learning experiences is best approached with an understanding of reflective and collaborative processes. The face-to-face classroom is collaborative before it is reflective. Its strength is in its spontaneity, which reinforces education as a social activity. It is a challenge to provide the time for students to reflect and offer a considered opinion. In fact, Abrams (2005) has found that students preferred a face-to-face environment but were more willing to critique participants' work in an online context because of the asynchronous nature of online learning. It is equally important that online learning be reflective before it is collaborative. The strength of online learning is the opportunity for reflection and rigor. It takes longer to compose a written message and communicate in a clear and concise manner that others will read and respond to. A community of inquiry would benefit from the integrated strengths of blending face-to-face and online learning and capitalizing on their inherent strengths.

Pedagogically, the CoI framework identifies the core elements and provides direction for the design of authentic and engaging higher-order learning experiences. For there to be a high cognitive presence, both reflection and collaboration must be present. Attention needs to be given to the opportunity for students to reflect on and monitor the construction of meaning, as well as to collaborate and manage the learning process. Students must be prepared and willing to recast their role. To benefit from a community of inquiry, students must be engaged both collaboratively and reflectively. Song and colleagues (2005) have shown that reflective thinking is perceived to be enhanced through collaboration. Blended learning offers the opportunity for all students to be cognitively engaged and feel that they are learning individually by participating in, and contributing to, a community of inquiry.

Conclusion

This chapter has provided an organizational framework to guide the exploration and understanding of blended learning. We began by identifying the characteristics of a learning community as being purposeful, open, and disciplined inquiry. To understand and shape the practice of blended learning, we described the CoI framework with its constituent elements—social presence, cognitive presence, and teaching presence. We argued that a community of inquiry is a unifying process that integrates the essential processes of personal reflection and collaboration in order to construct meaning, confirm understanding, and achieve higher-order learning outcomes.

Higher-order learning outcomes are the natural result of a purposeful, open, and disciplined learning process. Meaning cannot be imposed or "swallowed whole" (memorized), as Dewey

(1933) argues. It is the struggle of the individual making sense (constructing meaning) of the educational experience that is of lasting value. An educational experience is the transaction between teacher as pedagogue and subject expert and the engaged community of learners. The ultimate goal is not to acquire fragments of information but to collaboratively construct core concepts and schema based on important ideas and information. It is the understanding of the process of inquiry that will stay with the student and be of subsequent value in future learning endeavors. The best guarantee of quality learning outcomes is to focus on the foreground of the inquiry process with community and communication as the contextual background.

As noted in the introduction, blended learning is a simple concept but it is challenging in practice. In application it becomes a complex phenomenon and presents challenges in terms of disciplinary content, levels of instruction, and course goals. The complementary and reciprocal relationship of face-to-face and online learning offers the potential to rethink the educational experience. Blended learning is a fundamental redesign in which the combination of face-to-face and online learning represents a new approach and a qualitative shift in process and outcome. The fusion of real and virtual experiences creates unique communities of inquiry that are accessible regardless of time and location. If we did not already know that this was possible, it could be dismissed as simply an imaginative creation. We explore the practical realities of integrating the strengths of the real and the virtual experiences in subsequent chapters.

3

DESIGNING BLENDED LEARNING TO CREATE A COMMUNITY OF INQUIRY

New possibilities in the teaching and learning transaction begin with the flexibility of using and merging synchronous and asynchronous communication technologies. The principles and guidelines discussed here are based upon the assumption that the goal is to create a community of inquiry where students are fully engaged in collaboratively constructing meaningful and worthwhile knowledge. From both theoretical and empirical perspectives, there is little question as to the necessity and effectiveness of interaction and collaboration to achieve deep and meaningful learning outcomes (Garrison & Archer, 2000; Lapointe & Gunawardena, 2004; Oliver & Omari, 1999; Schrire, 2004).

At the heart of a meaningful educational experience are two inseparable elements of inquiry—reflection and discourse. In an asynchronous online learning experience, the advantage is given to reflection in a way that is not possible in the fast and free flowing face-to-face environment. The face-to-face classroom experience requires verbal agility, spontaneity, and confidence to express oneself in a group setting. Reflection and even interaction is greatly limited in most campus-based classrooms because of the number of students, along with dated pedagogical methods. Blended learning designs, however, recognize and capitalize on the properties of media and the potential to maximize the educational experience.

Interaction in and of itself is insufficient. Interaction must be purposeful and reflective. Students must be both stimulated and motivated to consider the essence of the material being presented, and then translate that into personal meaning that can be transmitted and validated. In a full educational experience this process is not left to chance. Educational experiences must incorporate the appropriate elements of design, facilitation, and direction of the educational experience. Through teaching presence, interaction is shaped into reflective and critical discourse. Schrire (2004) found that the presence of an active instructor moved online discussions to more advanced stages of inquiry compared to discussions led by students.

The primary challenge in a meaningful educational experience is to create and sustain a sense of community. Building community in a blended environment requires an understanding of the properties of synchronous verbal and asynchronous text communication and how to integrate these forms of communication to achieve desired objectives. Creating and sustaining this community is framed by the three essential elements of a community of inquiry—social, cognitive, and teaching presence—as discussed in the previous chapter.

In this chapter we describe the principles for creating and sustaining social and cognitive presence under each of the three descriptors of teaching presence—design, facilitation of discourse, and direct instruction.

Principles

Education is a structured learning experience designed to achieve intended outcomes effectively and expeditiously. The role of the educational leader is to provide the teaching presence that will structure, support, and shape a meaningful and worthwhile learning experience. Hence, considerable thought and care must be devoted to the design, facilitation, and direction of the learning experience. These tasks frame the following discussion about the educational environment from a blended learning perspective.

Design

Designing a blended learning experience is a daunting challenge. When designing for a face-to-face or online experience separately, the dominant mode of collaboration is either verbal (listening and talking) or text-based (reading and writing) communication. Educational designers must accept and adjust to the strengths and weaknesses of the medium. However, in a blended learning context, the designer is not limited by the communication medium. Although realistically there will be resource limitations, the educational designer has a broader range of choices. There is the potential and challenge to maximize the strengths of verbal and text communication for the particular experience, thus providing the opportunity for a complex weaving of learning activities and techniques from a full spectrum of possibilities.

The premise is that the ultimate goal is to create a community of inquiry in which learners are fully engaged and responsible. A blended learning environment offers the potential not only to create but to sustain a sense of community beyond the temporal limits of the face-to-face context. This means to extend the learning community over time and enhance the depth of engagement. Designing a blended learning experience entails taking special consideration of social and cognitive issues at the front end—issues that go well beyond deciding what content will be covered.

Social Presence. The goal of designing for social presence is to create a climate of trust and open communication that will support interaction and engender a questioning predisposition. Social presence is an essential precondition for establishing a sense of community and a cognitive presence.

PRINCIPLE: *Plan to Establish a Climate That Will Encourage Open Communication and Create Trust*

There is evidence of a link between design and establishing social presence (Swan & Shih, 2005; Tu & McIsaac, 2002). That is, courses that intentionally build a sense of community and collaborative activities will demonstrate increased social presence. Moreover, establishing social presence is associated with the degree of interaction among students (Beuchot & Bullen, 2005; Garrison & Cleveland-Innes, 2005; Tu & McIsaac, 2002). This would suggest that situations must be designed in which students have an opportunity to interact formally and informally with peers. This requires not only ice-breaker activities but also opportunities to engage in small-group discussions.

Establishing social presence appears to have an advantage in a face-to-face environment (Coppola, Hiltz, & Rotter, 2002; Fabro & Garrison, 1998; Garrison, Cleveland-Innes, & Fung, 2004; Rocco, 1996). Students perceive face-to-face and online learning environments differently. The face-to-face environment seems to focus students more on their peers and issues of social presence (Garrison, Cleveland-Innes, & Fung, 2004). Abrams (2005) found increased evidence of emotional support in the face-to-face environment that was absent in the online environment. The ability to see each other in a face-to-face setting should not be underestimated in providing "kinship" and students' identifying themselves as a group. Part of this is that the face-to-face environment allows participants to engage in familiar and immediate forms of communication (Vaughan, 2004; Vaughan & Garrison, 2005). Face-to-face interaction has significant advantages in the early stages of community building (group identity) and establishing trust to support collaborative learning. This trust can then be transferred to an online context (Rocco, 1996).

However, establishing and sustaining social presence are different challenges. Sustaining social presence can be accomplished efficiently online. In a purposeful educational environment, Vaughan (2004) found that social presence and students' needs shift from open communication to that of group cohesion, which encourages collaboration in an online environment. When designing instruction one should remember that communication for social presence in an online context is less frequent and more deliberate and intentional compared to a face-to-face context, where physical presence more naturally stimulates explicit expressions of social presence. Yet a face-to-face environment can also have a dampening effect on critical discourse and create an environment of "pathological politeness." Students are often reluctant and not prepared, from a subject matter perspective, to critique their peers (Abrams, 2005).

Cognitive Presence. Just as there is a link between social presence and a sense of community, there is also a link between a community of inquiry and learning (Rovai, 2002; Shea, Li, & Pickett, 2006). The design of academic activities has a significant impact on how students approach learning (Garrison & Cleveland-Innes, 2005). Shea, Li, and Pickett (2006) found an association between design, clear expectations, and a sense of community.

Building a community of inquiry is also important to incorporate legitimate academic tasks into the class rather than just focus on social issues. Community continues to build as we attend to the academic goals of the course. Cognitive presence grows as we inquire into the course content in a systematic and meaningful manner. Cognitive presence is defined by the process of inquiry that moves from problem definition to exploration of relevant content and ideas, integrating those ideas into a cogent structure or solution, and then directly or vicariously testing the validity or usefulness of the learning outcome.

PRINCIPLE: *Plan for Critical Reflection, Discourse, and Tasks That Will Support Systematic Inquiry*

From a design perspective, it is useful to consider how students perceive the face-to-face and online learning environments. When students were asked to anticipate their role adjustment to online learning from the perspective of an experienced online learner, students focused first on cognitive presence

(Garrison, Cleveland-Innes, & Fung, 2004). Online learning requires a cognitive and internal orientation. Marra and colleagues suggest that online discourse appears to be more task-related with "broader and deeper participation in group activities" (Marra, Moore, & Klimczak, 2004). Online learning appears to generate high levels of cognitive activity (Heckman & Annabi, 2005). Weigel (2002) suggests that written responses encourage a more integrated and deeper level of thinking. Thus, online "learning may be perceived as congruent with deep approaches and higher quality learning outcomes" (Garrison, Cleveland-Innes, & Fung, 2004, p. 70). However, a face-to-face environment may be more conducive to defining the task and negotiating expectations and responsibilities.

A study of critical thinking in a blended environment determined that face-to-face seminars created more new ideas but online conferences produced more important, justified, and linked ideas; that is, there was deeper critical thinking in online discussions (Newman, Webb, & Cochrane, 1995; Newman, Johnson, Cochrane, & Webb, 1996). Similarly, Meyer (2003) states that online "discussions were often more 'thoughtful,' more reasoned, and drew evidence from other sources" (p. 6). Asynchronous written (that is, online) communication is "an effective tool for promoting critical thinking through collaborative work" (Abrams, 2005, p. 38). The nature of face-to-face and online learning environments shape collaboration and discourse in distinctive ways. Abrams (2005) found that although students will critique anonymous authors in a face-to-face setting, they are reluctant to critique other members of the community. Meyer (2006) also found evidence that expressing dissent in person is much harder but may be valued more. The bottom line is that undergraduate students are concerned with offending their peers in a face-to-face context.

Schweizer and colleagues have shown that blended learning has an advantage for collaborative task performance (Schweizer, Paechter, & Weidenmann, 2003). The important point is that the effectiveness of the method of communication chosen (online versus face-to-face) depends on the type of task. Face-to-face communication appeared to support more coherent discussions and the solution of problems that required collaboration and the sharing of knowledge. Part of the explanation was the difficulty in maintaining coherence in online discussions. This difficulty, however, appeared to result from a lack of clear expectations (design) and guidance; that is, teaching presence.

It is our experience that the communication media do have different advantages. Therefore, educators need to consider which phases of an educational task are best conducted in an online or face-to-face environment. For example, more individual and reflective phases might be better served by employing an online context. That said, teaching presence in the form of design and facilitation has an enormous impact on the success of the educational experience and can overcome deficiencies in the communication medium. Even when operating in congruence with the strength of the medium, optimal teaching presence is required. We return to this theme in subsequent sections.

Hawkes and Romiszowski (2001) compared face-to-face and online dialogue and found that online dialogue was less interactive but had significantly deeper explanations. Garrison and Cleveland-Innes (2005) concluded that design had a significant impact on how students approach learning and that quantity of interaction was not a significant predictor of the quality of the learning experience. Moreover, Celentin (2007) revealed that quantity of interaction can in fact reduce the quality of discourse.

It would seem that having the opportunity to reflect before contributing to the discourse adds an important critical dimension. In a face-to-face context it is very difficult to reflect in action and keep all the facts and ideas current. The online environment also has the distinct advantage of providing a permanent record that students can use to reflect upon. The issue of reflective and permanent discourse is one to consider when deciding between face-to-face and online learning during each of the phases of inquiry. Well-designed online learning also demands that learners accept increased responsibility for their learning. Integrating the distinct strengths of face-to-face and online interactions may well optimize collaborative performance (Rocco, 1996).

Facilitation of Discourse

Discourse is the essence of a collaborative-constructive, that is, inquiry, approach to teaching and learning in higher education (Garrison & Archer, 2000). To ensure that students are meaningfully engaged and the discourse is rich and relevant, care must be taken to maintain a sense of belonging to the community of inquiry. The challenge is to sustain social presence while creating cognitive presence. This necessitates a strong teaching presence to know when and how to question and challenge students, and to know how to collaboratively guide discussion. Swan and Shih (2005) suggest that facilitating discourse requires the weaving of both social and cognitive presence. Online learners express higher levels of satisfaction and report higher levels of learning when they discern effective facilitation of discourse from their instructors (Shea, Fredericksen, Pickett, & Pelz, 2003; Shea, Pickett, & Pelz, 2003).

Social Presence. The goal is to enhance and sustain social presence that will provide the environment for collaborative and cohesive discourse. Social presence provides the foundation and the climate for learners to focus on intended learning goals. As social presence is established, it becomes less explicit (that is, tacit) as students engage and collaborate with their peers on the curriculum. This notion is supported by evidence that continued high social presence is most significantly associated with group cohesion (Swan & Shih, 2005; Vaughan, 2004). We suggest that group cohesion is important to sustain a community of inquiry in both a face-to-face and an online environment.

PRINCIPLE: *Sustain Community by Shifting to Purposeful, Collaborative Communication*

Trust and individual projection within a community are enhanced with frequent interaction and open communication. However, collaboration on a deeper and meaningful level requires a qualitative shift in interaction to focus on the shared purpose of the learning experience. The challenge, from a social presence perspective, is to maintain group cohesion and collaboration during critical discourse. Cohesion built upon the shared purpose of the learning experience is paramount. A cohesive community of learners is associated with higher-quality learning outcomes (Dixson et al., 2006).

The power of a blended learning design is that one can design face-to-face activities that lay the foundation for social presence. Online activities will then sustain social presence in the support of collaborative activities. From an online social presence perspective, students are always in virtual contact with their community, but they are physically alone at the computer. Their sense of independence is strong. As a result, online students do not manifest the same quality of social presence as they do in a face-to-face classroom setting (Vaughan, 2004; Vaughan & Garrison, 2005). The online experience, however, can maintain and enhance a sense of group cohesion, collaboration, and support—this reveals the value of a blended experience to both establish and sustain a sense of community.

From a facilitation perspective, it is important to recognize when to provide feedback to encourage the group to assume responsibility for purposeful discourse. The facilitator must also be cognizant of potential conflict or tension that may undermine the cohesion of the group. In addition to content expertise, the facilitator must have good interpersonal skills if the community of inquiry is to be sustained. It is a difficult balance to question and challenge, while ensuring that individual students continue to feel that they are contributing and are valued members of the community.

Facilitation is a blending of social and cognitive presences. In practice these elements are inseparable in a collaborative-constructive or inquiry approach to learning, and care must be taken to ensure that they are in dynamic balance. Students must feel safe to challenge ideas. Finally, social presence can have a qualitative influence on collaboration. Swan and Shih (2005) state that students "who perceive high social presence in the online discussions also believe they learned more from it than did students perceiving low social presence."

Cognitive Presence. Cognitive presence is the process of collaboratively constructing meaning and confirming understanding in a sustainable community of inquiry. Whether in a face-to-face or online context, facilitation is essential to keep the discourse on track and true to the evolution of inquiry. Facilitation focuses and guides the progression of the discourse, provides timely input and information, and summarizes development.

PRINCIPLE: *Encourage and Support the Progression of Inquiry*

The importance of facilitating discussion for a successful and satisfying online learning experience has been well documented (Benbunan-Fich & Arbaugh, 2006; Fabro & Garrison, 1998; Garrison & Cleveland-Innes, 2005; Shea, Li, & Pickett 2006; Oliver & Omari, 1999; Swan & Shih, 2005; Vaughan & Garrison, 2005). It is no less important to provide focus and progression in a face-to-face environment. The two contexts have different characteristics. The difference is the nature of the communication—that is, verbal versus text—as well as the physical presence of a teacher. Face-to-face discussion is fast-paced and fleeting, and structuring the discussion is a particular challenge. The facilitator must be cognitively agile by identifying important contributions, being energetic, moderating participation, identifying issues, and, since time is of the essence, knowing when to summarize and move on. On the other hand "time is expanded" in the online environment (Meyer, 2003). Online discussion is more accessible, more specific and detailed, more open to critical challenges and disagreement, and has increased potential for integration and resolution. Greater emphasis is placed on the facilitator to thread discussion, sustain commitment, encourage a conversational approach, provide relevant information links, and resolve issues.

As a collaborative community of inquiry moves to more challenging cognitive activities, facilitation becomes increasingly important to ensure that student contributions are acknowledged and constructive. For many students, online discussion forums are a new form of communication. Students will need encouragement and guidance to engage in the discussion. "Lurking" or vicarious participation may be an issue. Although participants can benefit from actively following the discussion, overt participation provides much more benefit from a critical thinking perspective. Sharing and testing ideas is a crucial phase of critical inquiry.

Facilitation has been shown to be crucial in modeling critical inquiry and sustaining cognitive presence. However, students must also feel they are contributing members of the community and must feel a sense of accomplishment. It is important for the facilitator not to dominate the discussion. This is a difficult balancing act for the facilitator because, on the one hand, students need to assume some control or ownership of the discussion. On the other hand, students want direction, and there are times when direct teaching presence is required.

Direct Instruction

Direct instruction is about academic and pedagogic leadership; that is, educational leadership that provides disciplinary focus and structure or scaffolding but also offers choice and opportunity for students to assume responsibility for their learning. This instruction is more than a "guide on the side" but less than a "sage on the stage." It is an approach whereby learning is socially shared. This is the path to a meaningful, systematic, and worthwhile educational experience. Students remain engaged and focused while achieving desired learning outcomes.

Social Presence. Direct instruction is counterintuitive in the sense that it can increase confidence, self-direction, and respect by managing potential conflict and ensuring that students are collaborating constructively. Direction is important for the group to remain productive and, therefore, to provide a stimulating context for individual development.

PRINCIPLE: *Manage Collaborative Relationships to Support Students in Assuming Increasing Responsibility for Their Learning*

A successful blended learning environment requires strong teaching presence to establish the climate for collaborative learning. In the face-to-face environment, leadership and modeling must be evident to establish a sense of community that will enable students to be comfortable and willing to share their thoughts. Because of time constraints in a face-to-face environment, students often have fewer opportunities to contribute to the discussion. In this regard, the immediate presence of the teacher makes it possible to intervene to control dominance or intimidation and build relationships. However, as students move to the online environment, the sense of community becomes more fragile. Students will have an increasing sense of independence. A direct teaching presence may be required to reinforce collaboration and a cohesive community of inquiry. It is especially important to intervene in a timely manner when inevitable tensions threaten the cohesiveness of the community.

Cognitive Presence. Direct teaching intervention is more natural and expected regarding cognitive tasks. As with most aspects of teaching presence, it is important to find the right balance. Too little direct teaching presence may see students lose focus and purpose. But too much direct intervention can undermine students' taking responsibility for their learning. The primary role for direct instruction is to ensure that discourse and collaboration evolve in constructive and purposeful ways.

PRINCIPLE: *Ensure That Inquiry Moves to Resolution and That Metacognitive Awareness Is Developed*

Recent research has begun to emphasize the importance of strong leadership to ensure that discussions stay "on task and on track" (Vaughan & Garrison, 2005). Inquiry is founded in a question-based approach. Although it is necessary for students to struggle with questions, there are times when direct answers need to be provided with regard to content or management of the process. Students value input when discussions are fragmented or floundering for lack of insights. It may mean providing a deeper explanation. Diagnosing misconceptions and providing explanations constitute an essential educational responsibility. Students must not be allowed to become frustrated to the point that they disengage. Direction may be needed from the subject matter expert to help students become aware of the nuances of the discipline. Confirmation of understanding often requires direct intervention. Moreover, appropriate intervention ensures that students experience success.

One of the areas of pedagogical interest is that research has shown that online inquiry may stall at the exploration phase (Garrison & Archer, 2006; Meyer, 2003; L. Rourke & H. Kanuka, unpublished). It would seem that communities of inquiry do not naturally progress from exploration to resolution. From one perspective this should not be surprising. The group dynamics literature has shown that groups often remain at one stage and do not progress fully to the performing stage (Tuckman & Jensen, 1977). More revealing is a study by Murphy (2004) of collaborative problem solving in an online learning environment. The participants in this learning community were specifically tasked to formulate and resolve a problem. Perhaps not surprisingly, participants did move through all the five problem solving phases. In fact, "participants engaged more in problem resolution than in problem formulation" (Murphy, 2004, p. 5). What this shows is that when the goal is to move to resolution (for example, problem or case based), participants will move beyond exploration.

Teaching presence in terms of design and facilitation is necessary to ensure that communities come together in a productive manner. Communities of inquiry do not automatically or quickly move to integration and application phases of inquiry unless that is the objective and a teaching presence creates and maintains cohesion. Cohesion is created through clear expectations and collaboration. Open communication and chat rooms are not sufficient in themselves to maintain a community of inquiry. Familiarity developed through sustained purposeful discourse creates the cohesion necessary for participants to progress through the phases of inquiry. Purpose and cohesion provide the motivation for participants to want to belong to a community of inquiry and remain committed to resolve educational tasks. However, this may not be enough to ensure that participants remain challenged and achieve intended goals. The other essential element in a purposeful community of inquiry is direct instruction.

Direct instruction has a legitimate place in a blended learning environment to ensure that the discourse, verbal or written, evolves in educationally appropriate directions. In a recent study, Shea and colleagues (2006) found that learners were more likely to report higher levels of connectedness and learning when they had online instructors who provided more "directed facilitation" toward the accomplishment of educational objectives. A key feature is the timely movement from discourse to resolution. This does not just happen by chance; it requires leadership and management. This was the conclusion of Meyer (2003) when she stated that faculty "may need to be more directive in their assignments for threaded discussions, charging the participants to resolve a particular problem, and pressing the group to integrate their ideas and perhaps, even, to prepare a resolution of the matters under discussion" (p. 8).

Although students expect strong teaching presence, too much direct intervention will most assuredly reduce discourse and collaboration. On the one hand, the risk in a face-to-face environment is that too much focus and responsibility shifts to the teacher. As a result, students' first choice inevitably will be to turn to the teacher for answers. Consistent with this, Heckman and Annabi (2005) found that face-to-face discussions were choreographed by the teacher, alternating between the teacher and a student in a linear, turn-taking manner. On the other hand, in an online environment the risk has been lack of structure and communication logic or coherence. Early in the emergence of online learning, the perceived democratic potential of asynchronous communication produced many advocates for less structure and the "guide on the side" approach. In an educational context, this posture was not always appropriate and left many students adrift and faculty confused and disillusioned. In both contexts, there are recurring situations that require more than facilitation and guidance.

Ultimately the goal is for students to become self-directed and to have learned how to learn. Achieving this goal necessitates the development of metacognitive awareness. Awareness of the inquiry process is essential if students are to assume increased responsibility for their learning, and the process may well be best introduced and explored in a face-to-face context. Online learning activities can provide an opportunity for students to reflect on learning tasks and strategies. However, online reflection requires a model of inquiry that can be used to assess learning strategies and judge effectiveness. The practical inquiry model that operationalizes cognitive presence can serve to increase metacognitive awareness (Garrison & Anderson, 2003).

Assessment

Finally, assessment is essential to any educational experience. It is also a very challenging responsibility. As Ramsden (2003) states, it "is about several things at once" (p. 177). Assessment informs both teaching and learning. It diagnoses misunderstanding, judges achievement, and provides feedback on the effectiveness of teaching methods. Assessment is further complicated in that it must be congruent with intended outcomes, the nature of the discipline, and student needs and abilities. It is no less challenging when blended learning designs are employed. However, a blended learning environment also provides additional options for effective assessment that can match learning activities and goals.

Assessment will inevitably shape how students approach the educational experience. The primary task in assessing learning is to ensure that assessment techniques support and enhance intended learning processes and outcomes. The intended learning outcomes in higher education are deep and meaningful learning. Achieving deep and meaningful learning is the primary motivation for adopting blended learning designs. Blended learning designs provide for sustained discourse and critical reflection. For deep and meaningful approaches to be successful, it is essential that students be assessed for their depth of understanding, not for simple factual recall. Blended face-to-face and online learning environments provide appropriate and constructive assessment venues.

PRINCIPLE: *Ensure Assessment Is Congruent with Intended Learning Outcomes*

From a formative perspective, assessment speaks to the importance of discourse to identify misconceptions. Here, the immediacy of face-to-face discussions may have an advantage in exploring false assumptions, concepts, or connections. The challenge, however, is to engage in deep discussion with all the students. Since there is a greater opportunity for participation, rigor of expression, and permanence of thought in the online environment, this may have an advantage for formative assessment. The online learning environment provides for reflection. To ensure that students have the time to reflect, caution must be urged with regard to over-loading students with information. With access to the Internet, there is considerable risk that information overload will result.

Conclusion

Although all of the teaching presence categories—design, facil-itation, and direction—are crucial for a successful educational experience, it is going to be very difficult to facilitate and direct the learning process without a clear purpose, structure, or plan of activities. For this reason, the first two principles associated with design consider how to *establish* social and cognitive presence. These principles will pretty much dictate what is to follow. The third and fourth principles address the issues of *sustaining* social and cognitive presence through purposeful activities. The fifth and sixth principles are associated with ensuring the *progressive development* of social and cognitive presence in a collaborative and constructive manner. These principles reflect the establishment, sustainability, and progression of social and cognitive presence. The last principle, assessment, serves to maintain the *accountability and credibility* of the educational process. It keeps the educa-tional process on track and identifies the inevitable need to shift focus or direction as learning develops.

For purposes of analysis, the various presences have been dis-cussed separately. However, this is an artificial separation, and we do not mean to suggest that one can discuss social presence in isolation from cognitive presence. If the goal is to create a community of inquiry, then we must consider the integra-tion of all the presences as contributing to a collaborative-constructive learning experience. For example, design will affect facilitation, and together they will have an enormous influence on cognitive presence. Similarly, in a blended learning context, it would be very misleading to think of either face-to-face or online learning. The challenge is to imagine the integration of the approaches and media to most effectively and efficiently achieve the intended learning processes and outcomes. It is not that particular learning activities cannot be effectively used in one medium or the other. It may be just too impractical from a cost or convenience perspective to create an intellectually stimulating environment and achieve the same levels of discourse and collaboration. The challenge of maximizing discourse in an efficient manner becomes evident when dealing with large classes.

In the end, however, blended learning is about fundamental redesign. It eschews being constrained by traditional approaches but considers and adopts the enormous potential of information and communication technologies. We must begin to break down notions of what is "real" and what is "virtual." The reality of the face-to-face classroom is that much of the discussion becomes vapor. On the other hand, ironically, the written discourse of the so-called "virtual" online classroom offers permanency and perhaps more opportunity for reflective and rigorous thought. Understanding the strengths of both face-to-face and online learning is the first step to being truly open to new approaches and technological possibilities. The principles described here will guide this redesign.

The task of designing a blended learning experience can be very challenging for an individual professor. We strongly suggest creating a community of inquiry for faculty to provide collaborative support. The next chapter offers professional development strategies based upon the CoI framework that can support faculty during the design process.

4

COMMUNITY OF INQUIRY FOR
FACULTY DEVELOPMENT

A recent survey of e-learning activity at 274 colleges and universities in the United States found that 80 percent of undergraduate and graduate higher education institutions and 93 percent of doctoral institutions offer hybrid or blended learning courses (Arabasz & Baker, 2003). Moreover, most institutions of higher education are being challenged with regard to the quality of the undergraduate learning experience and, as a result, are inevitably actively redesigning their courses and programs to integrate communication and Internet technologies (Twigg, 2003). When combined with projected faculty attrition rates, these developments create serious professional development challenges for higher education institutions.

Although the infusion of new faculty and the adoption of new communication and Internet technologies will most certainly have a positive influence in the long term, these institutions must concurrently facilitate the integration of new faculty into a complex set of roles and responsibilities. In essence, new faculty, who are themselves in transition, are being asked to integrate into an institution also in transition. This is of particular concern for teaching development and preparation of faculty to provide a quality learning experience. The greater proportion of new faculty in higher learning institutions have had little formal teaching development or experience. To compound this, pressure is being placed on these institutions to increase access to higher education, improve the quality of student learning, and control or reduce the rising cost of instruction. In this context, it is not difficult to appreciate the challenge for higher education and the importance of faculty support programs.

In response to these trends, many institutions have initiated faculty development programs to help the increasing number of new faculty prepare for their teaching responsibilities and be able to effectively integrate technology into their teaching practice. These programs usually involve technology training workshops, seminars, summer institutes, or project-based work with a production team to create a course Web site (Murray, 2002). A criticism of these types of faculty development initiatives is that they do not create opportunities for sustained critical reflection and discourse about one's teaching practice. A study by Rice and associates suggests: "New faculty want to pursue their work in communities where collaboration is respected and encouraged, where friendships develop between colleagues within and across departments, and where there is time and opportunity for interaction and talk about ideas, one's work, and the institution" (Rice, Sorcinelli, & Austin, 2000, p. 13).

Currently, the most common type of professional development is skill-based workshops, which attempt to train faculty in how to use a specific technique or software application. The difficulty is that faculty often come to these workshops and become enthused about the possibilities of using educational technology but then must return to their offices without the necessary time, or follow-up support, required to put their new ideas into practice. There is also a lack of opportunity for teachers to share their ideas, concerns, and frustrations with other faculty who are concurrently going through the same development process. Furthermore, the faculty members who do master these new skills often use educational technology to reinforce, rather than to change, existing teaching practices.

Cagle and Hornik (2001) suggest that another form of faculty development involves professional development institutes. These institutes usually range in length from a single day to a week-long event. There is often a project focus within these institutes with a mix of discussion and hands-on sessions. The advantage of such institutes is that there is time to clearly link theory to practice and to also create a sense of community and interaction among the participants. The downside of this approach is the lack of follow-up from such institutes, which often prevents the successful implementation of new teaching techniques and strategies. Recently, a greater emphasis has been placed on faculty development initiatives, which strengthen relationships among colleagues and support stated institutional goals (Camblin & Steger, 2000). Research by Lieberman (1995) also suggests that a collegial network is fundamental for effective professional development in education.

Slavit and colleagues state, "It is becoming very clear that professional development must be an ongoing activity, as 'shotgun' approaches often do little to promote real change" (Slavit, Sawyer, & Curley, 2003, p. 35). Thus, professional development programs should occur over an extended period, such as a semester or academic year, to allow participants time to transform their teaching practice. This leads to the concept from Mary Huber and Pat Hutchings (2005) about a teaching commons where "conversation about teaching and learning—informed by evidence and grounded in practice—can become the norm rather than the exception" (p. 32).

Blended Faculty Community of Inquiry

One example of a faculty development program that is typical of this new focus on community and a connection to an institutional mandate is the faculty learning community (FLC) initiative at Miami University (Cox, 2002). Cox (2002) states that a FLC consists of "a cross-disciplinary group of five or more faculty members (8 to 12 is the recommended size) engaging in an active, collaborative, year long program with a curriculum about enhancing teaching and learning and with frequent seminars and activities that provide learning, development, interdisciplinarity, the scholarship of teaching and learning, and community building" (p. 1). The participants in an FLC engage in a continuous process of reflection and discourse about complex teaching problems. There is constant support from colleagues throughout this process, but there is a focus on "getting things done" (Cox, 2004, p. 2). Survey data from the Cox (2004) study indicate that as a result of the FLC process, there is increased faculty interest in the teaching process (86 percent) and in their view of teaching as an intellectual pursuit (82 percent).

The major challenge of sustaining such communities is always one of time. Increased teaching and research commitments leave both new and experienced faculty with limited time for face-to-face professional development. Our experience suggests that a blended faculty community of inquiry (CoI) provides the necessary flexibility, structure, and organization to support and sustain the course redesign process (Vaughan & Garrison, 2006a). This type of CoI program attempts to model effective blended course practices and provide faculty with a hands-on blended learning experience through a series of face-to-face, online, and independent activities. The ongoing face-to-face sessions allow personal relationships and a sense of community to develop that fosters the sharing of ideas and experiences among the participants. The online component of the blended design creates an opportunity to extend and sustain this type of discourse and community.

The focus within a blended faculty CoI program is on the connection between one's teaching practice and student learning. The potential exists within such a professional development program for faculty to make a transformational shift in their approach to teaching from one of disseminating information to one of creating learning environments. Students are able to co-construct their own knowledge through interactions with the professor, their peers, and the course content. The role of technology shifts from the packaging and distribution of information (content) to its use as a "tool set" to enable students to communicate and collaboratively construct their own knowledge. Sands (2002) indicates that technology should be used as a catalyst to question one's curriculum and pedagogy. Garnham and Kaleta (2002) state: "The process of answering this question—'what will I teach online and what will I teach face-to-face?'—provides critical information about the discipline, content, teaching methods, learning processes, and the media and technologies available to support the most effective combination" (p. 3).

Voos (2003) echoes these comments by emphasizing that "when faculty re-design material they know deeply for a new delivery modality, breakthroughs are made in student learning, student satisfaction and faculty satisfaction" (p. 4).

Thus, a blended faculty community of inquiry should provide the time, support, encouragement, and recognition for participants to reexamine and reflect on their course curriculum, teaching practice, and use of information and communication technologies. This support usually comes in the form of a grant or award program such as the Inquiry and Blended Learning program at the University of Calgary (see http://tlc.ucalgary.ca/teaching/programs/itbl/).

Triggering Events

The triggering event for participation in a blended faculty community of inquiry is often the motivation to redesign an existing course to improve student learning and faculty satisfaction. This desire presents the opportunity to make one's implicit assumptions about a particular course explicit. The process can be initiated with a formal call for proposals to participate within a blended faculty community of inquiry. The application process should be designed so that professors are provided with a framework and the necessary support to begin examination of their existing course and to construct initial plans for the redesign process. Appendix Two contains the participant application form used at the University of Calgary for the Inquiry and Blended

Learning program. This form consists of three parts: project detail, project evaluation and sustainability plans, and a proposed budget. The University of Calgary facilitates a series of brown-bag lunches and one-on-one application consultation sessions to provide project-specific assistance and to ensure that faculty are clear about the course redesign focus of the program and the expectation that they become active participants within the blended community of inquiry. Faculty are also encouraged to take a team approach toward the redesign process within their applications. The team can consist of other professors who teach the selected course, as well as teaching assistants, graduate students, and others who provide course-related support such as subject area librarians.

We strongly recommend that the selection of successful applicants be made by an institutional committee, composed of faculty, student, and administrative representatives. These committee members should be familiar with the academic mission, goals, and strategic direction of the institution so that selections are made in alignment with these plans. On some campuses, a committee may already be in place, such as a Teaching, Learning Technology Roundtable (see http://www.tltgroup.org/programs/TLTR/home.htm). On other campuses, this type of committee may need to be created. At the University of Calgary, the Learning Instructional Development Sub-committee (LIDS), chaired by the associate vice president, oversees the Inquiry and Blended Learning Grant Program and selects the successful applicants from an annual call for proposals. There are ten annual awards for $10,000 and one $30,000 award for a major course redesign. The program is internally funded.

Once the successful applicants have been informed of their awards, we recommend scheduling an initial project meeting that includes the project team (professors, teaching assistants, graduate students) and representatives from the institution's teaching and learning center, library, and information technology department. The purpose of this meeting is to clarify the project goals,

timelines, roles, and responsibilities for those involved in supporting the redesign process. To effectively facilitate such a meeting it
is important to have a list of key planning questions, such as those
outlined in our Redesign Guide for a Blended Learning Course
(Appendix Three), to guide this initial course redesign discussion.
This meeting also helps identify needs for professional development support and requirements for the project team members.
This information is then used to shape the type of activities and
resources that will be incorporated within the blended faculty
community of inquiry.

As a follow-up to this meeting, we encourage the project
teams to post a summary message to a discussion board within a
course Web site that has been constructed for the blended faculty
community of inquiry. The message should describe the course
redesign goals for the project, action plans, and any questions
related to the redesign process (triggering events). This posting
helps clarify the course redesign process and also allows the other
members of the community of inquiry to learn more about each
other's projects. In addition, this process provides the first hands-
on opportunity for the participants to interact as students with
the learning management system that, in most cases, will be used
within their own projects.

The first face-to-face blended faculty community of inquiry
meeting should be designed to build upon the initial discussion
forum postings to allow the participants to further discuss their
course redesign questions and to also trigger new ideas and perspectives about teaching and learning. This process can be facilitated by selectively placing the participants into small groups so
that they have an opportunity to interact with people from other
project teams. Three questions that can be used to stimulate the
discussion are as follows:

1. What is your definition of blended learning and how will
   this concept be operationalized within your course redesign
   project?

2. What will be the advantages (for both students and professors) of your course redesign?

3. What do you perceive will be some of the challenges you will encounter with your project?

We have found it useful to have an instructional design or teaching specialist facilitate each small group discussion to help guide the discussion and to also record the key points. These discussion summaries can then be placed within the blended faculty community of inquiry Web site as a resource and "touchstone" to stimulate further online discussion.

Our experience suggests that the initial face-to-face cohort meetings are very important for establishing the blended faculty community of inquiry. Through the discussions within these meetings the community members realize they are not alone in experiencing a particular course redesign issue or concern. This shared understanding and physical presence of the participants can very quickly lead to a sense of "trust and risk taking" within the group.

Exploration

The exploration phase of the blended faculty community of inquiry should consist of a series of integrated face-to-face and online experiential learning activities that allow the participants to become immersed in a blended learning environment to see it from a student's perspective. We recommend that this process should take place over an extended period (a minimum of six months) and that the activities should be developed based on the feedback from the initial project meetings and in collaboration with the participants of the community of inquiry. Appendix Six provides an example of a planning document that can be used to develop activities for a blended faculty community of inquiry. We suggest that the cohort activities be designed to provide participants with experience and expertise in curriculum design,

Figure 4.1 Program Outcomes for a Blended Faculty Community of Inquiry

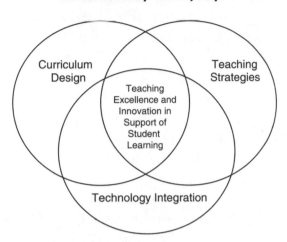

teaching strategies, and educational technology integration (Figure 4.1).

The curriculum design sphere involves the creation of a course outline or syllabus for the blended learning course. This document becomes the "blueprint" for the redesign process. To develop teaching strategies it is recommended that the program provide opportunities for the participants to develop experience and skills with online discussions, group work, and computer-mediated assessment practices. The educational technology integration component includes the acquisition of strategies and skills for managing a course Web site and trouble-shooting basic student technology issues.

To achieve these program outcomes there should be a variety of learning opportunities that allow participants to share, discuss, and debate their course redesign experiences. Experiments with the use of a variety of information and communication technologies can be conducted to support the exploration phase. For example, Adobe Presenter can be used to create brief audio presentations to help the participants prepare for an upcoming face-to-face session, explain an online activity, or summarize a key course redesign concept. Faculty research and travel commitments mean that not everyone can attend each of the regular face-to-face sessions. To overcome this challenge, Web-based synchronous communication tools, such as Elluminate Live!, can be used to record the face-to-face sessions for future use. Also, this type of tool can support "virtual" project meetings when team members are off campus.

We have also found it to be very effective to include faculty mentors (professors with previous blended learning experience) and students in many of the discussions. The students provide the all important perspective of the learner (target audience for the redesigned courses) and the faculty mentors are able to pass on their "lessons learned" from direct experience with blended learning courses. Previous participants of blended faculty communities of inquiry have also stressed to us the importance of conducting these discussions in both face-to-face and online formats (Vaughan & Garrison, 2005). The face-to-face sessions, with their physical presence and sense of immediacy, help establish the rhythm for the community, whereas the online discussion forums allow for reflective thoughts and comments to be captured and archived as project-related resources.

Integration

A common challenge we have observed for many participants involved in a blended faculty community of inquiry is the transition from the exploration to the integration phase. Most people are comfortable sharing, discussing, and debating course redesign concepts but often find that a greater effort is required to transfer these new ideas into practice. One strategy that we have found effective involves getting participants to regularly present project artifacts, such as a course outline or assessment activity, to the community. This forces the participants to make redesign decisions and to create course-related resources. This "show and tell" process also allows them to get valuable feedback from their peers about the artifact. In addition, opportunities should be provided to pilot portions of the projects with students who can provide insightful comments about the use and educational value of the learning activity.

To support the integration phase, we recommend conducting a series of individual project meetings outside of the regular cohort meetings. These meetings should be facilitated by an instructional design or teaching specialist who is assigned to specific projects, based on the area of expertise, to correlate with the predetermined support requirements for the project. The frequency and scope of these meetings depends on the needs of each individual project. While the larger cohort meetings provide opportunities for participants to be exposed to a diversity of ideas (breadth), the focus of these meetings is on "getting things done" (depth). Project development work and milestones can be reviewed at each meeting, with tasks and "deliverables" assigned for the subsequent meeting.

Application/Resolution

The application and resolution phase of the blended faculty community of inquiry involves the implementation and evaluation of the course redesign project. This is the phase that is often overlooked in professional development programs. In many programs, faculty receive support for the design and development of their projects, but the implementation stage takes place after the program has been completed. Thus, professors are left on their own to struggle through the initial implementation of their course redesign, and in most cases, little or no evaluation is conducted to determine the effectiveness of the project from either a student or faculty perspective.

To overcome these deficiencies it is recommended that the blended faculty community of inquiry be maintained throughout this phase and that the participants be intentionally engaged in the process of the scholarship of teaching and learning (SoTL). Hutchings and Shulman (1999) provide the following summary for this type of scholarship. They suggest that effective teaching involves a high level of proficiency to stimulate students and to foster their learning in a variety of appropriate ways. Scholarly teaching also involves evaluating and reflecting on one's teaching and the student learning that follows. The scholarship of teaching shares the characteristics of both excellent and scholarly teaching. In addition, it involves investigating questions relating to how students learn within a course or discipline, and communicating and disseminating the teaching and learning practices of one's subject.

To facilitate this process we recommend conducting a discussion about the SoTL process in one of the early face-to-face meetings of the blended faculty community of inquiry. These conversations should involve faculty mentors with prior SoTL experience who can demonstrate their study processes and results. We encourage faculty to engage in the scholarship of teaching and learning from the outset of their project. By applying for institutional ethics approval at the beginning of the course redesign process, project teams are able to collect data in the form of classroom observations, surveys, interviews, and focus groups from students, professors, and teaching assistants who have been involved in past iterations of the course. In addition, data regarding student grades and success rates (drop or withdrawal) can also be obtained from an institution's office of institutional analysis. The collection and analysis of this data combined with a thorough review of the existing SoTL literature for a particular course or discipline allows the project team to make informed course redesign decisions, that is, proper selection and integration of face-to-face and online learning activities.

Although each course redesign project will have its own specific scholarship needs and research study design, we also recommend applying for ethics approval for the entire blended faculty CoI program so that a common set of data can be collected for each of the project implementations. Analysis of these data can be used to inform future offerings of the redesigned courses and also to create an institutional course redesign inventory that can be used for academic program planning. Two sets of data collection techniques that are recommended for each project implementation include an end-of-semester student survey (Appendix Five) and a post-delivery interview with the professor and teaching assistants responsible for the redesigned course (Appendix Six).

The survey asks students why they selected a blended course, the amount and quality of the interaction, issues around course design and expectations, the most and least effective aspect of the course, and overall satisfaction. Appendix Seven provides a summary of the results from our initial implementation of this survey. The most significant positive finding was the expressed increase in the quantity and quality of interaction with both students and faculty. In terms of the amount of interaction, there was a 78 percent increase in the amount of interaction with other students and a 55 percent increase with instructors in these inquiry and blended learning (ITBL) courses (Vaughan & Garrison, 2006b). With regard to the quality of the interaction, the students reported that there was a 69 percent increase in quality of interaction with other students and a 59 percent increase with instructors. Previous studies at the University of Central Florida (Dziuban, Hartman, Moskal, Sorg, & Truman, 2004) have indicated that these perceptions of increased interaction are strong indicators of student success in a course. Comments from the student surveys suggest that group work was the primary reason for this increased interaction in ITBL courses. The students also indicated that group work, discussions (both face-to-face and online), and online resources were the most effective aspects of the redesigned courses.

In terms of the least effective aspects of the ITBL courses, the survey comments identified unclear expectations, online components, and heavy workload (Vaughan & Garrison, 2006b). Students were confused about course expectations, not prepared for online interaction, and surprised by the workload. Although students liked the group work, they felt they needed more guidance and structure. As a result of the perceived lack of organization, only 48 percent were satisfied with the course experience and only 45 percent indicated that they would take another blended course if given the opportunity. We discuss strategies for addressing these issues in Part Two of this book.

The post-delivery interviews provide an excellent opportunity for the project teams to reflect and debrief about the redesigned courses (Vaughan & Garrison, 2006b). Questions such as "What worked?" "What didn't work?" "What to do differently the next time the course is offered?" as well as lessons learned and advice to other faculty contemplating course redesign are explored. The project team is also asked to reflect on their blended faculty CoI experience and provide suggestions to improve the program.

Preliminary analysis (themes and comments) from our initial interviews (see Appendix Eight) suggest that as a result of the implementation of the redesigned courses, professors have a greater awareness of the need to provide students with an explicit orientation to inquiry and blended learning, a "clear course plan," and ongoing direction throughout the semester (Vaughan & Garrison, 2006b). They also state that there is a greater need to align the student assessment activities with the course objectives and to focus more on discipline-specific inquiry rather than on just covering course content.

In terms of their blended CoI experience, the faculty interviewed indicated that the face-to-face lunch sessions provided them with "breadth" and opportunities to learn about diverse approaches to inquiry and blended learning, whereas the online components allowed them to reflect on how these new ideas could be incorporated into their own course redesigns. The optional workshops facilitated hands-on opportunities to develop learning resources for their courses, and the individual project meetings provided depth through discussions about project-specific issues, as well as the establishment of project milestones and tasks.

The process of course redesign for blended learning is still a relatively new phenomenon; thus it is important to disseminate the results and lessons learned from course implementations that have been supported by a blended faculty community of inquiry. At an institutional level, this dissemination can occur by creating opportunities for project teams to present their results on course redesign implementation to new CoI cohorts, at departmental meetings, and at institutional forums on blended learning. Articles can also be written and published within institutional newsletters, journals, and magazines.

Additional funding is often required to support the dissemination of implementation results beyond the institution. Opportunities for external dissemination often include academic journals and presentations at regional, national, and international conferences. The University of Calgary has recently created an Inquiry and Blended Learning Scholarship Dissemination Grant Program to support such activities (see http://tlc.ucalgary.ca/simple_teaching_program/inquiry_blended_learning_scholarship_dissemination_grants). Faculty who have been part of the blended faculty CoI program are eligible to apply for ten annual awards of $1,000. This grant is intended to directly support expenses related to designing, conducting, and publishing research on teaching innovations related to the inquiry and blended learning projects, and for travel to present a paper at a conference based on the results of a study that describes lessons learned in the course redesign and implementation.

Campuswide Initiatives

A blended faculty CoI program is usually created to provide course redesign support to a select group of professors, but we believe that it is also important to create a series of professional development opportunities that are available to everyone on campus to support and raise the profile of blended learning at an institution. One popular method is to organize plenary sessions or day-long events where blended learning experts are invited to speak and interact with the faculty on campus. In order to avoid these being "one-shot" events, we recommend organizing pre- and post-activities. Related papers and publications by the guest speaker can be placed on a Web site before the event. For example, see "E-Learning the Millennial Generation: A Blended Approach" (http://tlc.ucalgary.ca/community/stories/ elearning_the_millennial_generation_a_blended_approach). The actual presentations can be recorded and then linked to the Web site for future reference. For examples, see Dr. Carol Twigg (http://tlc.ucalgary.ca/community/stories/blended_learning _expert_visits_u_of_c); or Dr. Curtis Bonk (http://tlc.ucalgary. ca/community/stories/flattening_blending_and_harmonizing_the_ learning_envir- onment). Online forums, weblogs or wikis can also be used to facilitate ongoing discussion between the experts and the faculty. If the speaker has created a major blended learning resource or book, such as *The Handbook for Blended Learning* (Bonk & Graham, 2006), the potential exists to create an online study group with the author and interested faculty on campus.

As mentioned previously in this chapter, workshops are probably the most common form of professional development activity for blended learning, but they suffer from a lack of follow-up or support for faculty. To overcome these deficiencies, we recommend "mini" workshop series with follow-up opportunities such as individual, group, or departmental consultations. These workshop series usually consist of two to three related sessions where the focus is on providing participants with an opportunity to develop teaching strategies and resources that are specific to their course needs. Topics for these workshops should be based on the key course redesign issues encountered by faculty, such as designing an interactive course syllabus, managing and assessing group work, and engaging students in large class settings. Follow-up consultations can consist of meetings or classroom observations where feedback is provided about the implementation of a course redesign strategy that was developed within the workshops.

In addition to plenary sessions and workshops, we also found it to be useful to develop a series of "tip sheets" for faculty regarding common course redesign issues that have been experienced on our campus (see http://tlc.ucalgary.ca/resources/library). These two-page tip sheets are available in print or in a Web-based format, and they focus on connecting theory to practice for a particular issue. Each tip sheet introduces and gives the rationale for a specific teaching strategy, discusses the technique or tool, describes concrete examples of how this concept can be incorporated into a higher education course, and provides a list of related resources. Currently, we group our tip sheets into the following categories: teaching strategies, creating community, facilitating effective online discussions, assessment, e-learning tools, and organizing and formatting your course Web site. These tip sheets are created in partnership with professors from our blended faculty CoI program, and many of them create links within their course Web sites so that their students can easily access the tip sheets as learning resources. For example, the Orienting Students to Blended Learning tip sheet is widely used by students within blended learning courses. We also recommend creating an inquiry and blended learning (ITBL) wiki resource for your campus (see http://www.seedwiki.com/wiki/inquiry_through_blended_learning _resources). This wiki provides a venue for all faculty members at an institution to share and discuss course redesign resources and issues. We have divided the ITBL wiki into ten key topic areas:

1. Inquiry

2. Blended learning

3. Inquiry through blended learning

4. Course redesign

5. Learning outcomes

6. Teaching strategies

7. Communication and information technology tools

8. Assessment

9. Student orientation

10. Impact

For each topic area we provide links to related articles, resources, and tip sheets. We also strongly encourage our faculty to post artifacts from their blended learning courses such as course outlines, assessment activities, Adobe Presenter presentations, student surveys, and focus group instruments. Faculty have commented that they appreciate this ability to easily share and use resources that have been developed by their colleagues.

Conclusion

Course redesign for blended learning is a very challenging process, especially when undertaken in isolation by a single professor. Without the systematic and sustained support of a professional development community, individual faculty often make decisions about course redesign that do not harness the transformative potential of blended learning. For this reason, we have emphasized in this chapter an approach to professional development that focuses on the blended faculty community of inquiry. Such an approach allows professors opportunities to

- Reflect, discuss, and make decisions about their course redesign process with their peers
- Experience a blended learning environment from the student perspective
- Implement and evaluate their own blended learning courses with the aid of instructional design and evaluation support

We have also demonstrated that this type of professional development support, which emphasizes a community of inquiry framework, can be further extended across campus through the use of plenary sessions, mini-workshop series, tip sheets, and an inquiry-through-blended-learning wiki.

With this chapter we conclude Part One of this book and the discussion of the community of inquiry framework. We now move to Part Two and the practice of designing blended learning environments. In the next chapter we attempt to orient the reader at a macro level to typical blended learning designs.

Part Two

BLENDED LEARNING
IN PRACTICE

5

SCENARIOS

Having good models and successful exemplars is essential for widespread change. Higher education faculty are professional critics and skeptics. Faculty must be able to see what the possibilities are. When most faculty see their colleagues successfully innovating and receiving recognition, they will not be far behind and will be extremely motivated to keep up with the competition. This is why we begin this section with some good examples or scenarios in order to convey a reasonably concrete image of what blended learning might look like.

In this chapter we provide various models and concrete examples of three distinct course redesign scenarios and challenges. The focus is on instructional design approaches, various strategies and tools, and implementation issues. The following scenarios are organized within three types of redesign challenges faced by institutions of higher education. Each of the scenarios reflects successful blended learning designs associated with types of courses common in higher education. They cut across disciplines and are an amalgam of the best features and examples of course redesigns based upon our experiences and those found in the literature. Each redesign scenario addresses specific needs and seeks an optimal balance between face-to-face and online learning activities to achieve the intended educational goals.

Small Class Courses

The first two scenarios describe modest blended learning redesigns that could apply to a large number of small to medium-sized, second- or third-year undergraduate courses taught by a single professor. These redesigns are open to most professors with little financial investment. All that is needed is an understanding that the learning experience could be enhanced with new approaches to teaching and learning and the utilization of ubiquitous information and communication technologies such as the Internet and learning management systems (LMS). The academic goal is to create a sustained community of inquiry that extends beyond limited classroom opportunities. The primary goal here is to reduce lecturing while increasing inquiry and discourse. Although to enhance the quality of learning is the primary goal, conveniences and efficiencies are gained through reduced lecture time. Efficiencies gained can be reinvested to enhance the quality of the learning experience. For example, the professor has more time to engage in student discourse and feedback. In addition to reduced commuting time, students focus on more meaningful learning activities.

Political Science

The first scenario of a basic small-class, blended learning redesign is a second-year political science course with a limited enrollment of fifty students. The course is an introduction to public policy studies and the problems facing governments in initiating, formulating, enacting, and implementing policy. The course was traditionally delivered via three one-hour lectures per week supported by extensive handouts (no textbook). Students had two major assignments and a final exam. Case studies were used, but discussions were dominated by the same four or five individuals. To print and distribute class materials was an administrative challenge. The professor thought that it would be a barrier and confusing to students to place everything in the LMS. Students were also limited in accessing optional materials or very large policy documents, an inherent challenge in a course like this. Although the professor had recently introduced an online discussion forum, it was not well received and was very time consuming. Even though 5 percent of the students' grade was allocated for participating in online discussions, students were resistant. The students regarded the activity as just another task on top of an already content-heavy course. Students complained that there were too many messages, they were too long, and the discussion was fragmented and often irrelevant because of little facilitation.

The first challenge of the redesign was to find a means to engage students in more meaningful discourse. The assumption had been that students would naturally find the discussions interesting and of value. The reality is that students associated their participation directly to assessment. The premise was that if the discussions were crucial to the course, then time had to be made for student interaction. The solution was that three lectures per week were reduced to two. Most important, however, students were prepped for online discussion in the first lecture of the week with the introduction of case studies. More effective use of case studies was achieved using online discussions that required reflection and well-crafted written discourse. These discussions were moderated by the professor. The professor received professional development guidance to effectively manage an online discussion, such as creating smaller groups, and to manage time. Guidelines were provided for the students regarding the nature, frequency, and length of messages. Credit for online discussions was increased to 10 percent of the final grade. Finally, all course documents—for example, outline, expectations, and readings—were placed in the LMS for easy access.

The goal to involve the students in more meaningful and sustained discourse was achieved. Student evaluations revealed that students found the discussions not only interesting but also that 80 percent of the students agreed that the online discussions contributed to a better understanding of the course content. Two key reasons for this were that discussion took place in both large and small groups and the professor was present but did not dominate the discussion. The other key achievement that the students appreciated was the access to a wide range of relevant and current documents so essential to the course.

Philosophy

The second scenario of small class redesign is a third-year philosophy course with an enrollment of approximately thirty students. The course is on metaphysics and comprises four major topic areas: the realism/anti-realism debate, causality, freedom versus determinism, and the relationship between the mental and the physical. Originally the course had two ninety-minute seminar sessions per week supported by a collection of academic journal articles. The assessment for the course consisted of four short papers, one for each key topic area. The professor responsible for the course was discouraged with these short paper assignments. She indicated that students were not demonstrating understanding of the connections among the four topic areas within their papers, and that these assignments took a great deal of time to read and assess. In addition, the professor was also frustrated with the nature of the seminar discussions. Students were not reading the assigned articles before they came to class, the classroom comments lacked insightful reflection, and the discussion was often dominated by one or two opinionated students.

The focus of the redesign was to create a course structure, which would enable students to make deeper connections between the four main topic areas. This was accomplished by revising the student assessment requirements, using an electronic portfolio system, and reducing the amount of class time to one, ninety-minute seminar per week. The number of student papers required for the course was reduced from four to three. Students now had the choice to select one of the four major topics for an individual short paper and an additional topic for a collaborative group paper. In addition, each student wrote a final capstone paper, which synthesized the four topics. The papers were uploaded into an electronic portfolio system and students were required to use the weblog feature, a journaling tool, within this system to provide reflective comments on their papers. These comments included insights about how the papers connected to the major course topics and the lessons learned for future assignments. Students also used the wiki, a collaborative writing tool, within the electronic portfolio system to create and comment on their group papers. The single weekly class period was now used as an opportunity for the professor to discuss misconceptions in writing she had observed within the electronic portfolio system and for the students to share, debrief, and plan their individual and collaborative writing assignments.

The student evaluations and comments from the professor indicate that the goal of creating deeper connections between the course's major topic areas was realized. The professor indicated that the quality and connectedness of the students' papers increased dramatically and that the reduction in the number of assignments combined with the use of assessment rubrics significantly decreased the amount of time she had to spend on grading. Students stated that the use of the electronic portfolio system and the introduction of the group assignment facilitated a greater sense of meaningful engagement with the course material and their peers "inside and outside of the classroom."

Large Enrollment Courses

Large enrollment courses provide what may be the quintessential opportunity for blended learning redesign. There is invariably a strong need to enhance the quality of the learning experience accompanied by a great opportunity to gain cost and convenience efficiencies. Large classes invariably rely on the lecture with the misperception that this is the best that can be done with limited resources. The reality is that the lecture is a poor means to engage students with the content, even when presented in an entertaining manner. Moreover, from the professor's perspective, it is time consuming and generally an unpleasant challenge to prepare two or three lectures a week. There is little connection or interaction for the students with peers or the professor. Students endure the experience to get the credit, and faculty long for release time so they can have more time for their research—the primary activity that is recognized and rewarded.

The next two scenarios address what is perhaps the greatest challenge facing higher education today—providing an engaging and meaningful learning experience to students taking high-demand introductory courses while recognizing the ever present fiscal constraints of higher education institutions. The first scenario describes a high enrollment communications and writing course that was previously offered through multiple sections. The second scenario is a high-enrollment chemistry course conducted by large lectures. The goal of both scenarios was to enhance the learning experience in a cost-effective manner.

Communications and Writing

The purpose of the communications and writing course was to introduce first-year students to communication theory and the principles of oral and written communication. The course was previously taught in three, one-hour lectures per week with an optional tutorial. Assignments, such as projects and presentations, asked students to produce various forms of oral and written communication. The course was originally delivered in 25 sections with 20 students in each class. Each of the sections was taught by either a part-time instructor or a senior graduate student. The challenge was to find a more effective and efficient design by providing for less time sitting passively in lectures and more time actively engaged in writing. It was also important to have the presence of a senior professor.

The goal of this redesign was to address variances in quality across sections. The first step was to place a professor in charge of quality assurance and the overall design and delivery of the course. Efficiencies were gained by providing a single lecture per week. The weekly lecture was complemented by one-hour weekly tutorials led by a teaching assistant (TA), online peer-to-peer collaboration, and individual access to the professor. Online resource materials and a question forum, which included examples of papers and projects, resulted in increased efficiency and effectiveness. Students were provided increased flexibility and convenience as a result of fewer lectures and more online learning activities. The online activities also encouraged students to be more actively engaged in their learning between lectures.

Efficiencies and consistency were also gained in not having 25 instructors prepare their lectures independently. The professor, TAs, and an instructional design consultant formed a supportive team to manage this redesign project. Training was also provided to all instructional staff as to how to structure and facilitate online discourse and respond to questions effectively and efficiently. This initial investment of resources experienced a return after the first offering of the course. During the second offering adjustments were made to communicating expectations and explaining shifts in responsibilities. Students were pleased with the increase in collaboration and support materials. Instructional staff were pleased with the division of responsibilities and the flexibility in terms of time provided by asynchronous online facilitation. It should also be noted that the combination of online materials and collaboration, including the informal sharing of paper drafts, resulted in the submission of better quality papers and less onerous grading of papers. Fewer grades were appealed, which saved the professor's time in having to regrade those papers.

Chemistry

The second large-enrollment redesign was an introductory chemistry course. The purpose of the chemistry course was to provide an introduction to inorganic and organic chemistry from a theoretical and practical perspective. The course had an enrollment of between 500 and 600 students. Students were grouped into two sections and received two eighty-minute lectures per week. Each section of the lecture had 250 to 300 students and was taught by one professor and two teaching assistants. Students also had a three-hour lab each week. The TAs managed aspects of grading and the lab. Questions outside the classroom were handled by the TAs. Large lectures and diminishing resources created a serious barrier to active and collaborative learning and interaction with faculty. In its simplest terms, the challenge was to increase the quality of the learning experience and to reduce the high student failure rate. Students simply did not engage with the content.

The goal of the redesign was to address the quality of the learning experience by giving fewer lectures and more meaningful learning activities. The redesign was led by two professors with sustained support from an instructional design and technology perspective. The first step in the redesign was to eliminate one of the lectures and replace it with online tutorials, help rooms, and resources, as well as increased opportunities to engage the professor or TAs for individual help. The approach to the weekly lecture was also fundamentally redesigned. The lecture no longer simply transmitted information with the purpose of "covering" the curriculum. Instead, it was used to introduce concepts from a problem perspective and explore their practical implications. This was facilitated through the use of a digital classroom response system. A problem would be posed by using a PowerPoint slide, and students would individually, or in teams, be given time to solve the problem. They would then "vote" on the correct response by "clicking" on their hand-held, wireless control units. Subsequently, the audio component of these lectures was captured in synchronization with the PowerPoint slides and then placed on the course Web site for subsequent review by the students. The use of these digital technologies encouraged the professor to be more focused during the lectures, and they also allowed students to access and replay these conceptual discussions outside of class time.

Online tutorials were designed to complement the lectures and provide additional background materials, example problems, additional problem-solving opportunities, and other activities. Students received immediate feedback during these tutorials. Weekly wet labs were reduced to once every two weeks. Online dry labs were required in the alternating weeks. The dry labs were not created specifically for this course. It was far more cost-effective to acquire online tutorials and tests from a commercial publisher. Students were also assigned to face-to-face tutorials moderated by a TA. The tutorials were integrated with an online help room where students could get help from peers and TAs in a timely manner. There were also online self-assessment and practice quizzes to provide formative feedback and diagnosis of conceptual deficiencies. These were used to indicate to students when they were prepared to take a bi-weekly online quiz that constituted 20 percent of the course grade. Finally, there was a class Web site where the course outline, course content and links, and assignments were posted. Students could receive updates from the Web site and the professor could address questions that surfaced in the subgroups.

The greatest benefit of this redesign was the significant reduction in the rate of withdrawal and failure. This was attributed to a more engaging and effective redesign. Students were encouraged to assume greater responsibility and were provided better guidance and feedback. Cost savings from the redesign features, such as reduced frequency of lectures and fewer repeats, were reinvested back into the course by way of increased student accessibility to, and interaction with, the professors, TAs, and online learning tutorials and labs.

Project-Based Courses

The focus of this scenario is on courses with educational goals not amenable to large lecture approaches but requiring increased access. New approaches need to be adopted that can maintain the integrity of a small class yet meet increasing enrollment demand cost-effectively. The solution lies in some fundamental rethinking of the design and delivery of the course from a pedagogical and structural perspective.

Scientific Writing

The scientific writing course was originally taught in a traditional lecture-based manner—three lectures and one lab each week. Although course documents were submitted electronically to the instructor, the system was managed via e-mail. This process was incredibly time-consuming, limited the number of students that could be accommodated, and reduced the time possible for one-on-one interactions with the students.

The course targets undergraduate science students, although it is open to students from all faculties. Students are primarily in their second year of university, but the course is also open to third- and fourth-year students. This course originally accommodated twenty to thirty students per year. The redesigned course is now able to accommodate 100 students per year.

The redesign of this course was based on three important goals: (1) to increase the time available for individual writing process consultations with students, (2) to create course materials that support a new inquiry-based, student-driven approach to scientific writing, and (3) to ease the administrative workload for the instructor.

Students hone their writing skills by completing four scientific papers. Before each paper is submitted for grading, it is subjected to a peer-review process. Students complete a paper on a given topic and submit it to a teaching assistant and two of their peers for review. The comments give students an opportunity to substantially revise their paper before it is handed in for grading. Originally, the movement of documents was handled manually. This created an overwhelming amount of administrative work for the instructor and severely limited the number of students that could be accommodated in the course.

Guided by student comments, the course was redesigned to include a series of seven lectures on key aspects of scientific writing, an integrated and significant library research component, and a comprehensive Web site that supports student learning. Individual student consultations replaced structured lectures, and students were afforded more time to research, write, and review papers. Faculty now had more time to engage students in one-on-one discussions. The key technological innovation that ensured the success of this project was the development of a document management system called the Peer Review Tool (PRT).

The document management system is an Internet-based tool designed to automatically manage document flow throughout the peer review process. When a student submits a paper the tool automatically sends it to his or her classmates (anonymously if desired) for review. Once the reviews are complete, the file is again submitted to the management tool and is automatically sent back to the original author. The tool allows documents to move through the peer-review process with little involvement of the instructor. This gives the instructor more time to interact with the students because less time is spent administering the process. Since documents are uploaded and retrieved from the same Web site, students can see when their paper has been successfully submitted. The free Calibrated Peer Review (CPR) tool developed at the University of California Los Angles can also be used to facilitate this process (http://cpr.molsci.ucla.edu/).

Instructors report that the quality of students' writing improved throughout the semester and the time spent in administration and document management was considerably reduced. The course serves as a successful example for further initiatives in the science area.

Nursing

A second radical redesign is a nursing course whose purpose is to provide for advanced clinical practice through adult and higher education teaching and learning approaches. This course was previously offered in the late afternoon in a traditional one-and-a-half-hour lecture twice a week. Class sizes ranged from thirty to forty students. The first challenge for this course was that of student access. Most students were working and found it very inconvenient to travel to campus. The timing of the class was also problematic, as those working the day shift were tired and the class was inaccessible to those working an afternoon shift. The second challenge of the course, which was designed for students to critically analyze teaching approaches and strategies and for transforming clinical educational practice, was the students' lack of engagement in the discussions and therefore the unsatisfactory quality of those discussions.

The course was redesigned to begin with a Saturday workshop. The purpose of the workshop was to provide the students an intensive introduction to the course and to other students in the class. Expectations were clarified and negotiated. Students then attended monthly face-to-face evening seminars conducted by faculty. Students were assigned to two seminars with a maximum of 20 students. Continuity was provided by well-structured online activities, assignments, and discussion forums. Teaching assistants facilitated online discussions with the direct supervision of the professor. Lectures were presented online through a synchronous communication system such as Elluminate Live! along with extensive reading and resource materials. Small-group (two to three students), collaborative, online assignments were designed. Students were also asked to take the lead in moderating discussions in the seminars, as well as discussions online between seminars, thus gaining an opportunity to apply techniques being studied.

This redesign significantly increased access to the course. As a result, more practicing nurses were able to benefit from the course. Most important, students expressed strong satisfaction with the course in terms of the quality of engagement with other students. Students were given the opportunity to share experiences and insights from their practices. This was shown to be the most valued learning experience from the students' perspective. Faculty found that the quality of the discourse increased dramatically as well. Faculty indicated that this method of delivery was less onerous and more satisfying than previous course offerings.

Conclusion

In this chapter we identified three typical course redesign challenges and offered concrete examples of each. The first set of redesign scenarios—small class courses—focused on fewer lectures and sustained, asynchronous communication to design more engaging and meaningful learning experiences. The second set of redesign scenarios dealt with large undergraduate introductory courses. This is the type of course that may have the greatest initial benefit from blended learning redesign by increasing both interaction and meaningful problem-solving. Considerable efficiencies are also gained with the adoption of new approaches to teaching and learning. The third set of redesign scenarios, project-based courses, focused on high-demand, low-enrolment courses. Access and collaborative learning opportunities were the primary challenges.

We now move from general blended learning scenarios to more specific practical guidelines in Chapter Six. In addition, Chapter Seven provides a more detailed explanation of the strategies and tools highlighted within this chapter.

6

GUIDELINES

Previous discussion focused on the broad pedagogical principles for blended learning design. This chapter offers guidelines for strategies and techniques to engage students in a blended learning environment. The core challenge is to create and sustain a purposeful, open, and disciplined community of inquiry. Building a blended learning community requires an understanding of the properties of synchronous verbal and asynchronous text communication, as well as a method to fuse these forms of communication to achieve intended learning outcomes. The guidelines derive from deep and meaningful approaches to learning, that is, they focus on organizational frameworks and concepts, and more specifically, from each of the previously identified redesign principles.

The blending of face-to-face and online approaches provides enormous possibilities. Variability is multiplied in a blended learning environment. The distinctiveness of each blended design is both the power and the challenge of blended learning. In this chapter we provide a more detailed roadmap to the design of effective and efficient blended learning environments. By identifying the properties of face-to-face and online learning approaches, we gain an appreciation of the atypical nature of blended learning designs.

New Approaches

The synchronous and asynchronous connectivity and collaboration made possible through blended learning designs portend a transformation of teaching and learning in higher education. Blended learning has become the catalyst to rethink traditional approaches and rediscover the learning community. Blended learning designs offer disciplined inquiry through reflective and collaborative activities, while providing unlimited access to information.

Technology is the integrating platform that seamlessly connects the real and virtual educational worlds. Much has been made of the changing attitudes and expectations of current higher education undergraduates. They are often referred to as the net generation (Net Geners). They do not make the same distinctions between the real and virtual worlds as did previous generations. They are able to move easily between face-to-face and online experiences, depending on their needs. The majority of undergraduate students are relatively sophisticated users of communications technology. For this reason, it should not be surprising that they are skeptical about the uncritical adoption of technology in higher education. In a recent survey of higher education students, Kvavik and Caruso (2005) found that Net Geners want technology to add convenience and connection but have only a moderate preference for technology. They also found that students value interaction and are concerned that technology will further reduce communication with their instructors.

It would seem that students perceive the instructor as crucial to the quality of the learning experience. As one Net Gen learner states, "Many Net Geners often leave the computer screen craving actual conversation and interaction with their instructors" (Windham, 2005, p. 46). The same Net Gener suggests that students want to learn through exploration to understand the steps taken. That is, they do not want to be burdened with facts, but want to be engaged with the content and with other students. Finally, she adds, the "professor must be an active participant and facilitator" (Windham, 2005, p. 52). This new generation of students is embracing the flexibility and relevance of blended learning educational experiences and environments.

The selection and integration of media must be shaped by educational goals and design considerations. Although technologies may have strengths and weaknesses that must be considered, ultimately it is teaching and learning considerations that will have the most direct influence on learning. Technology can expand possibilities through the support of various forms of communication, but it is the design of the experiences and how students are engaged that directly affect the quality of the learning experience. The technology of synchronous and asynchronous connectivity, synonymous with blended learning, may offer previously unimagined options. This potential, however, will not be realized without practical guidelines to inform design decisions. Blended face-to-face and online learning approaches can only be integrated successfully with an understanding of fundamental teaching and learning processes.

New approaches must not be based simply on the medium of communication or even the nature of the environment, whether real or virtual. A quality higher education learning environment is characterized by a purposeful, open, and disciplined community of inquiry. Although we are able to describe the basic elements and processes, we are still challenged to design the conditions that seamlessly integrate face-to-face and online learning and engage students in a deep and meaningful manner. What is required to develop higher cognitive and metacognitive abilities? Some of the best insights into this question are provided by the literature on deep and surface learning.

A focus on the quality of learning outcomes and processes has revealed two basic and distinct qualitative approaches to how students perceive and approach learning—deep and surface approaches (Marton & Saljo, 1976). A deep approach to learning, on the one hand, is an intention to comprehend and understand the meaning and significance of the subject at hand. Content is purposefully organized into meaningful structures. Surface approaches, on the other hand, have unreflective, rote, and fragmented learning strategies. Typically this is a strategy adopted by students when the quantity of learning is rewarded over the quality of understanding. Deep and meaningful approaches to learning focus on organizational frameworks and concepts, as opposed to disparate facts and data.

From an educational perspective, deep and surface approaches to learning are concerned with designing educational environments with the express purpose of achieving higher-order learning outcomes. The premise is that the context shapes how students approach their learning. The two most important elements in shaping approaches to learning are assessment and the amount of content (Ramsden, 2003). First, students will approach learning in the way that it is rewarded. That is, if you test for recall only, students will approach learning in a surface-learning manner. If you wish students to approach learning in a deep manner, then students must be engaged in discourse and collaborative tasks. However, students will have little chance to approach learning in deep and meaningful ways if they are overwhelmed with content and do not have the opportunity to discuss, reflect, and digest the meaning of the material presented.

The teacher can influence student perceptions and approaches to learning with the design and management of the context. That is, the quality of learning outcomes is, to a large extent, influenced by the educational designer and the learning community. The possibilities of blended learning may well present a potentially ideal higher education environment for the collaborative construction of active, deep, and meaningful learning.

Applying the Principles

The following discussion of more specific guidelines is organized around the principles discussed previously in Chapter Three. The first two principles were associated with design of social and cognitive presence. We next explore the guidelines associated with that design.

Design

The challenge of designing for social presence is the establishment of a climate that supports open communication within a community of inquiry. Guidelines associated with this principle aim to establish trust among the students through interaction. The goal is to create trust that will support open communication and a willingness to collaboratively engage within a community of learners. An example of an activity to establish a climate for openness and collaboration is each participant introducing himself or herself and sharing concerns about the course expectations. The focus is equally on connecting with other students and collaboratively understanding how the course will be conducted. An opportunity to negotiate formal expectations of the course should be included in this activity.

Negotiating expectations may be done best in a face-to-face context, but it can also be done effectively online. It is also important to create a "chat" room for informal communication to encourage student familiarity and personal relationships. This will increase students' comfort level and confidence to engage in more academic discourse. Similarly, a static learner-profile area that contains brief student-authored biographical information that is available for easy and ongoing reference would increase social presence. It may also be appropriate to share a digital picture.

Whether face-to-face or online, students should be assigned initially to small groups to discuss formal expectations of the course and identify concerns. This will concurrently focus students on the purposeful nature of the community, as well as allow for more interaction and a growing sense of belonging. Group spokespersons could be selected to share the views of the small group in the main discussion forum. This is a good opportunity for the teacher to establish the climate for discourse by modeling respectful exchanges. Not only must students get to know each other, but the teacher must also get to know the students. To an appropriate degree, teachers should allow students to get to know them if they are to be perceived as a member of the community. Finally, online office hours also contribute to the formation of a community.

Inquiry necessitates a trusting and supportive classroom climate. Climate setting is important for both face-to-face and asynchronous online learning environments. In a face-to-face context there is considerable anxiety and a perceived risk in challenging ideas and engaging in critical discourse. Discourse is not common at the undergraduate level and will require some time and effort to establish social presence. In an online learning environment, however, some students may feel less inhibited. Because of the asynchronous nature of online communication, it is easy for individuals sitting alone in front of their computers to be less inhibited. Although online communication can encourage communication that is more open than in a face-to-face situation, respect must be established for members of the community.

The guidelines for designing cognitive presence are to establish opportunities for critical reflection, discourse, and collaboration in support of systematic inquiry. The first important guideline is to seriously consider course content from an inquiry perspective. If collaboration and discourse are to be at the core of the inquiry process, students must have the time to engage other students and reflect upon their deliberations. Activities should be problem-based and question-driven to engage the students in reflective discourse. For example, discussion should be focused on activities such as finding solutions to problems and resolving case studies, or alternatively, on students working on projects.

An important goal of an inquiry approach is to create opportunities for small group discussion. It is essential, in the very early stages of the course, that an opportunity for substantive, curriculum-focused discourse be provided. A brainstorming exercise, or non-threatening questions such as "what do you think of . . .?", may be appropriate in the early part of the course. In a face-to-face context, an instructor-led discussion early in the course is appropriate so that students do not feel pressured to "perform" in front of their peers. For this reason, it may be advantageous to concurrently engage students in an online discussion early in the course of studies. Again, small-group discussion opportunities provided early in the course of studies allow students to engage more actively and with less anxiety. As groups report back, it is important that the teacher respond, model respectful discourse, establish a friendly environment, and reinforce the guidelines for discourse. This will help set the stage for subsequent team-based collaborative projects. For either face-to-face or online discussion, the more clearly the instructor instills students with an understanding of the value of a culture of collaboration, the more likely it is to develop.

As noted previously, excessive workloads and inappropriate assessment techniques can negate inquiry and deep approaches to learning. It is important that students be provided choice and be given time to reflect on the key concepts. Great care should be taken in selecting reading materials and the method by which students will be assessed. If individual readings and assignments are excessive, motivation will limit engagement in online discussions, regardless of marks given for participation. However, face-to-face activities must mesh with online activities. Rupert Wegerif (1998) reports that there is evidence to suggest that collaborative activities may be better supported online. For example, topics may be introduced face-to-face, and interest generated, before moving to online discourse and assignments.

Online activities can become onerous and excessive because they may seem ever present, and some students expect immediate and continuous responses. This relentless pressure can be an issue if clear expectations for length of messages and guidelines for how often participants are expected to respond remain unclear. Also, written discourse is more rigorous and therefore time consuming. Another issue is that collaborative performances are enhanced by both online and face-to-face commitments, but expectations and time commitments can also expand. Again, consideration must be given to the workload required.

One of the challenges in collaborative learning is to ensure that students continue to progress through the phases. Activities should be designed that encourage students to move from awareness to knowledge construction and finally to application. Beyond community building and climate setting, the early exploratory phase of inquiry may have some advantages in a face-to-face environment. For example, brainstorming can have a motivational advantage in a spontaneous and energetic face-to-face environment if the goal is to generate lots of ideas. On the other hand, if the goal is to generate quality ideas, an online learning environment would be the better choice. Rocco (1996) demonstrated that brainstorming in an online context was superior to that in a face-to-face context if the object was seeking solutions. Ideally, of course, one could integrate both by initiating the brainstorming in a face-to-face environment and then having participants refine their contributions online.

Finally, a design stage guideline is to seriously consider the role adjustment for students in terms of operating in both the face-to-face and online environment, as well as changing expectations in terms of being more active and responsible for one's learning. New approaches and membership in a community of inquiry will be a significant adjustment for most students. The expectations of inquiry and discourse in general, as well as how this translates to face-to-face classroom interactions compared to online written discourse, must be clear to students. The adjustment may be particularly enhanced in the online context if students do not have online experience. They must not only understand their role but that of the teacher or moderator. It must be clear that the teacher is there to facilitate, not to dominate the discussion.

Facilitation

The guidelines discussed next are associated with the facilitation of social and cognitive presence.

Facilitating social presence means to sustain community by shifting from initial efforts at open communication to nurturing purposeful cohesive responses. Cohesion sustains a community of inquiry. Group cohesion is necessary for students to engage in discourse and collaborative activities. Cohesion is an extension of the initial establishing of trustful and open communication necessary to create a community of inquiry. It helps participants focus on the mutual goals of the community and results when participants recognize and commit to the community's intended purpose. This places considerable responsibility on the facilitation of the learning process. For cohesion to be sustained, discourse and collaborative activities must be facilitated to ensure that participants engage productively with each other.

Sustained discourse and collaborative activities provide the best means to build and maintain group cohesion. A face-to-face classroom environment may be a good context to introduce a topic and focus interest. However, students must have extended opportunities to construct meaning and confirm understanding. This is often best done online. Facilitation is the challenge in an asynchronous online context to maintain cohesion and productivity. The facilitator must create the conditions and assist students to actively contribute to the discourse. Once again we recommend small breakout groups to ensure strong participation and commitment to the group. The facilitator should allow these groups to operate in anonymity to encourage free discussion without somebody judging their contributions. A member of the group reports back to the larger group.

In a face-to-face setting, personal and socio-emotional ties may be generated more quickly. At the same time, in a face-to-face environment, personal relationships may interfere with honest critique. Although students find increased personal support and camaraderie in a face-to-face context, it can also inhibit discourse. Abrams (2005) found that a face-to-face educational environment produces reluctance or unwillingness to critique fellow students. Similarly, Meyer (2006) found that in a face-to-face setting, students appear to have a higher concern for hurting others' feelings, but they are more willing to disagree with other students in an online environment. Personal connections can enhance cohesion and the motivation to persist in collaborative learning activities. However, too much emphasis on the social and emotional ties can provide a false sense of cohesion that may undermine the educational purpose and the function of a community of inquiry.

The online learning environment may have advantages in engaging students in academic discourse and reflection. In an online setting, social presence becomes more subtle as the course progresses. Cohesion is very much sustained through purposeful discourse and recognition of mutual goals. Although there is a clear and respectful connection to the community, the focus is on ideas and mutual understanding. Participants are less inhibited to express themselves. However, tensions may result that undermine cohesion. A good facilitator must be aware when passion may threaten cohesion and the productivity of the group. Cohesion is essential for cognitive presence and sustaining a community of inquiry.

Guidelines for facilitating cognitive presence encourage and support the progression of inquiry through to resolution. Suggested guidelines are to provide stimulating questions, keep discussion focused, identify issues needing clarification, and be prepared to move discussion forward in a timely manner. Facilitation in either a face-to-face or online environment is absolutely essential to focus discussion and ensure it moves beyond the exploration phase.

Facilitation may take on a slightly different approach in a face-to-face environment compared to the online environment. As noted previously, listening is largely an information-acquisition activity, and talking is a sharing of ideas and information. From an inquiry perspective, the face-to-face listening and talking activities may be best suited to introducing and exploring problems or issues. Participants in a community of inquiry should be given considerable freedom to brainstorm and share information and experiences. However, at some point the divergent discussion needs to become more focused and some order created. It is at this stage that discipline and reflection are important attributes. The online environment may have an advantage at this point, especially with large classes. Writing may be better suited to document and integrate key ideas. This is a more challenging phase of inquiry and the discourse must be productive in searching for a solution and resolution. Although the role of facilitation is challenging in both contexts, the responsibilities vary as students move through the inquiry cycle.

Learning activities that take advantage of listening and talking should be considered for the face-to-face context. For example, lecturing, brainstorming, role playing, and debate are interesting and powerful learning activities in a face-to-face environment. They rely on rapid verbal and visual exchanges. Activities for online learning experiences use discussion forums, case studies, or article critiques. Although these activities can also be successful in a face-to-face context, the online environment adds opportunity for reflection and rigor to the discourse. In addition, all students have an opportunity to contribute. Case studies are based upon a real-life situation, and all students have a chance to share their experiences. Students are able to respond to other student contributions and systematically build upon ideas offered by members of the community. The role of the facilitator is to model and thread the discourse.

As students gain experience, they should be given the responsibility to moderate a discussion. This opportunity has the advantage of generating commitment and raises metacognitive awareness. Although they may lack some of the subject matter expertise, they will gain a much better understanding of the inquiry process and become more responsible, self-directed, and proficient learners. However, a facilitator or moderator must have an understanding of the goals and the process required to reach the goals. It has been shown that students by themselves may not have the ability to weave discussion threads that lead to integration and resolution (Schrire, 2004).

Direct Instruction

The guidelines organized around the next two principles are associated with direct instruction. Facilitation is more of a guide and less of a leader. However, an educational experience also requires leadership. Direct instruction provides the leadership necessary for a worthwhile and efficient learning experience. Social presence associated with direct instruction is concerned with managing collaborative relationships to ensure students assume responsibility for their learning and not become distracted by personal relationships.

The instructional guidelines require the teacher to be supportive but expect that students will be self-directed and work collaboratively to complete tasks. From a group dynamics perspective, there will be a phase at which tensions and conflicts arise.

Tension is a natural and even necessary condition for critical discourse—personal conflict is not. Direct instruction is important to address these situations, clarify misunderstandings, and intervene when necessary. It may require a willingness to negotiate expectations or to correct a student who uses excessive or inflammatory language. However, the teacher must not be expected to resolve every minor disagreement. Students should be encouraged to address and resolve their own conflicts. Direct instruction does not include intimidation. Input and correction must be given with sensitivity and respect. Students must feel that they can question the teacher without retribution.

Students very much value and desire face-to-face communication and the reinforcement of personal relationships. Camaraderie grows as communities move into the "performing" stage. Activities should be created that strengthen the commitment to the community of interest. Face-to-face collaboration gives students the opportunity to connect personally while accomplishing assigned tasks. Small group assignments provide opportunities to share thoughts and experiences and develop camaraderie, which strengthens the community. Consideration should be given to maintaining subgroups for extended periods to allow students to get to know each other and provide personal and academic support.

Cognitive presence guidelines associated with direct instruction ensures that discourse moves to resolution and that metacognitive awareness results. Instructional guidelines associated with cognitive presence must contribute ideas and perspectives that constructively shape the discourse. Direct instruction may be required to offer alternative ideas and perspectives, respond directly to queries, suggest connections, and summarize discussion. Another key responsibility of direct instruction is to diagnose misconceptions so as not to let students get side-tracked and frustrated. Misconceptions need to be diagnosed and leadership given to assure that educational goals are achieved. To ensure progression through to resolution, a number of interventions such as shaping discussion through questions, setting and revising objectives, and summarizing may be required to move on in a timely manner.

The need to be directive in threading discussions in order to progress through the phases of inquiry is well stated by Meyer (2003), who argues, "Faculty may need to be more directive in their assignments for threaded discussions, charging the participants to resolve a particular problem, and pressing the group to integrate their ideas and perhaps, even, to prepare a resolution of the matters under discussion" (p. 8). The need to be directive in terms of summarizing and synthesizing is an important responsibility if difficult issues are not to be neglected. Jim Hewitt (2005) states, "To make disciplined, on-topic progress, participation must maintain a sense of the entire thread and the goals of the discourse" (p. 583).

At the same time, particular care must be taken with direct intervention. Too much direct instruction can discourage students from taking responsibility for approaching learning in a deep and meaningful manner. Students will simply look to the teacher for the answers. Teaching presence, even in terms of direct instruction, does not mean a teacher-centered approach. It should be noted that too little intervention is also a serious problem. Students may get off-track and either lose valuable time or lose commitment to purposeful collaboration. Both extremes put the community of inquiry at risk. Responsibility and self-direction must be encouraged at all times through leadership and good management of learning tasks.

Collaborative assignments and team projects encourage students to take responsibility and design learning strategies. If expectations and guidelines are clear, team projects can offer opportunities to engage in relevant, realistic problem solving. Through collaboration, students recognize the need for leadership, set goals, plan and manage tasks, assess progress, and adjust strategies where necessary. They begin to develop self-directedness and strategic planning. Other activities that foster responsibility and self-direction include student-authored learning journals where learners reflect on their learning processes and outcomes. Appropriately designed learning journals can foster reflection to allow students awareness of and strategies for the process of collaboration and its impact on their learning.

Responsibility and self-direction enhance metacognitive awareness. Garrison (2003) argues that metacognition has two dimensions. The first dimension is the ability to internally monitor one's knowledge and motivational states. The second dimension concerns external self-management and regulatory skills directed at resolving a problem or issue. Metacognition is an essential ability in learning to learn. An important insight here is the role of discourse and collaboration in modeling and sharing cognitive experiences. Sharing one's thinking, and monitoring and managing learning strategies in collaboration with others, can only increase reflection and metacognitive awareness. A community of inquiry is particularly suited to reveal metacognitive knowledge and strategies and to encourage self-monitoring and management of the inquiry process.

Making thinking explicit and open to deeper examination is a great advantage in increasing metacognitive awareness. The great advantage of online learning is that it makes a permanent record of thinking and therefore offers an opportunity for reflection and increased awareness of the inquiry process. Advantage should be taken in the online context to have students monitor and manage their approaches to learning through discourse and collaborative activities. In a face-to-face classroom context, enhancing metacognitive awareness in fast-paced and ephemeral verbal discourse may be practically impossible. It would virtually necessitate constant interruptions or a one-on-one tutorial. Yet the classroom environment is an excellent place to introduce the practical inquiry model and explore with the students the process and why it is important to be aware of how to monitor and manage one's learning.

An excellent practical technique to ensure that discussion progresses to the latter stages of the inquiry process and to reinforce metacognitive awareness is to have students self-code their postings. This would identify the level of the response and help students assess whether they are contributing to the discourse and moving the discussion to resolution. Pawan and colleagues suggest that the "strategy would encourage students to keep track of and to think about how their responses relate to the collaborative learning objectives set by their instructors" (Pawan, Paulus, Yalcin, & Chang, 2003, p. 137). To reinforce this, the teacher must model the behavior and code students' responses. They should also provide some metacognitive commentary of what they are doing and why.

The literature has shown that deep approaches to learning have been associated with metacognition (Entwistle, McCune, & Hounsell, 2003). To encourage deep approaches and to enhance metacognitive awareness, the expectations for deep and meaningful approaches to learning must be made clear to students.

Although assessment and volume of content affect how students approach learning, ultimately the challenge is to shift students' understanding of the learning approach. Students reveal their thinking through discourse and are encouraged to develop their metacognitive awareness and understanding of the inquiry process. As noted previously, assessment practices are crucial to shaping awareness and approaches to learning.

Assessment

Assessment cuts across all teaching presence categories. It may well be the most pervasive issue in designing a deep and meaningful learning experience. The guidelines associated with assessment focus on the principle of ensuring that assessment is congruent with intended learning outcomes.

Formative assessment is important to gain feedback regarding the success of teaching methods and techniques. In a collaborative constructivist environment, it is inevitable that explanations, directions, and methodological adjustments will need to be made as difficulties and new issues arise. In both face-to-face and online environments, minor or less urgent adjustments can be accomplished with direct intervention. However, when adjustments are more significant or complex, they may best be addressed in a face-to-face setting.

Summative course evaluations are critical for maintaining the credibility of blended courses. Moreover, summative evaluation is important to attain the integration and balance of face-to-face and online learning opportunities in a blended course. Designing a course for blended learning should be viewed as an ongoing process, since the tendency to "layer on" another learning activity is always present. In addition, the nature of the course assignments and the associated student workload need to be constantly monitored to ensure that assessment is congruent with the intended learning outcomes. Summative course evaluations are crucial to receive the necessary feedback to incrementally improve the design and success of the blended course.

Blended learning provides a diversity of options for assessment techniques. The online environment creates opportunities for students to demonstrate and share evidence of their learning through papers, electronic portfolios, project reports, and practice tests. The digital nature of these learning artifacts also allows for student and peer involvement in the evaluation process. Documents may be shared with peers for informal input before final submission or to form part of the assessment. There may also be benefits for a student self-assessment to form part of the final mark. Self-assessment can also encourage and enhance metacognitive awareness. Completing exams online is an option, but invigilation of formal examinations has an obvious advantage in the face-to-face context.

Serious thought should also be given to assessing discourse, especially online. Although this is a common practice, it is a complex issue and the advantages and disadvantages need to be weighed carefully. The argument in favor of grading discussions is that it provides incentives to participate and gives recognition to the efforts to engage constructively in the discourse. Philosophically, the downside is that you are providing extrinsic reinforcement to what should be an intrinsic academically reinforcing activity. If questions and issues are relevant to course goals and assessment and are interesting and well moderated, is there a need for extrinsic rewards? Assessing discourse may undermine students' taking ownership of the discourse, and they may see it simply as an exercise for a mark. Students will simply go through the motions and effectively place limits on what might have been learned and the quality of the outcomes.

Although arguments against evaluating online discourse may come across as being naïve, rewarding discourse also brings with it the practical challenge of grading discourse fairly and making it a learning experience. This can be extremely onerous. If it is deemed that assessing the quality of the discourse is worthwhile, it is essential that criteria and a grading rubric be provided as to how discourse will be assessed (see Chapter Six). This must be more than simply counting the number of postings. Such information guide students and provide the structure for a meta-discussion about the process and gains in metacognitive understanding. A rubric and metacognitive understanding of online discourse will help students understand the feedback they may receive from peers or the instructor.

Evaluating online discussions demands a clear set of criteria consistent with the desired outcomes. Based on the work of Knowlton (2003), we offer the following list of criteria for evaluating online discussions. Contributions should

- Be clear
- Be factually correct; cite assigned readings
- Offer critical thinking and analysis
- Be respectful
- Inspire further discourse; develop the scope of the discussion
- Contribute to the thread of the discussion

These criteria represent a starting point, depending on the nature of the discourse and the discipline. Along with the criteria a rubric is needed that links the criteria to observable elements of a contribution and a rating scale.

Assuming that critical thinking and discourse are the intended goals, consideration must be given to the stage of the discourse. For example, if the discussion is at the exploration phase, students should be given more latitude for divergent thinking, longer messages, and perhaps less-focused contributions. It is also important not to evaluate students harshly in terms of the formality of their writing style. Although clarity is important, students should be encouraged to explore and formulate ideas. Not unlike face-to-face discourse, the nature of online communication should reflect some rigor of thought but be conversational in tone.

For example, do postings encourage reflection and provide insights, do they engage others collaboratively, do they logically connect to other postings (threaded), and are they respectful of the community? Well-constructed online discussions have a degree of built-in peer evaluation. However, it is important to provide instructor feedback in the form of sustained facilitation and direct instruction when required. This feedback should assist in assimilating course content as well as gaining insight into the process of critical thinking and discourse. Discussion of the process itself will enhance metacognitive awareness and ultimately the ability of students to think and learn.

Conclusion

Our goal in this chapter was to explore practical blended learning guidelines that will support and enable the construction of meaning and confirmation of understanding in ways that exceed print or verbal communication independently. To this end, we have provided guidelines associated with each of the principles provided in Chapter Three. However, Entwistle and colleagues remind us that an educational environment "is a complex composite of many interacting influences that need to be aligned towards supporting deep active learning" (Entwistle, McCune, & Hounsell, 2003, p. 104). This is particularly true with regard to the design of blended learning environments, which add to the interacting influences the additional options and choice of fusing face-to-face and online communities of inquiry.

Notwithstanding the potential of learning technologies, online learning, on its own, has not come of age on traditional, campus-based institutions. Online learning has flourished within distance education institutions whose tradition and mandate are to make education accessible. For the campus-based institution, the challenge is to resist using new media to replicate deficient practices of the past. It is now time to step back and examine how we might integrate the potential of online learning with the traditional strengths of face-to-face learning. In the next chapter we move beyond guidelines and look at specific strategies and tools that can be used to design a blended learning experience.

7

STRATEGIES AND TOOLS

To this point we have provided the theoretical framework, principles, and guidelines for the design, facilitation, and direction of blended learning. In this chapter we offer the reader the strategies and tools necessary to engage students in a collaborative and reflective blended learning experience. The categories of teaching presence, as described in previous chapters, provide the structure for the practical ideas and tips that we give here, such as a blended learning syllabus, lesson ideas for the first week, discussion forum activities, and assessment rubrics. These strategies and tools can be readily adapted to a range of disciplinary contexts.

Planning and Design

Technology can be a catalyst and a means to adopt more active learning approaches. However, it is the educational design that guides the selection of appropriate strategies and tools. Blended course redesign requires a willingness to step back and consider the goals and range of possible approaches, strategies, techniques, and tools.

The challenge of integrating face-to-face and online learning, and the transformative nature of blended designs, argues strongly for the guidance of an instructional design specialist. Blended learning is not conducive to a prescriptive instructional design template. In design one must consider particular goals, the audience, and the context. Also, design must be flexible in coping with changing needs. This is not an easy task, but it can be exciting and engaging when completed in partnership with an instructional design specialist and other individuals involved with the course (that is, faculty, staff, and students). The course redesign team must have a deep understanding of the possibilities. Although there are few rules, there are key guidelines.

First, reconceptualize and redesign the entire course. Start fresh! Simply adding on to questionable approaches and designs is not sustainable and it does not enhance the quality of the teaching-learning experience significantly. Discard the obsolete, ineffective, and inefficient practices. Achievement of the potential of blended learning will require a critical rethinking of what we do and why.

Second, manage the volume of content. Consider the proliferation of information and the ability to access it. We cannot cover "all" the content in virtually any area of study, so difficult educational decisions are required. Perhaps, most important, students need time to reflect and process content. Too much content becomes a barrier to deep and meaningful learning. The focus must be on helping students create or understand knowledge structures (schema) that encourage deep and meaningful learning.

Third, create a community of inquiry. This capitalizes on what we know about a higher-order learning experience and the properties of communication and Internet technology to support interaction and discourse. A community of inquiry will engage learners and provide feedback to assess critical thinking (that is, cognitive presence). One can think of blended learning as a new "learning ecology," to use the phrase of Brown and Duguid (2000). Interactive and reflective capabilities create a community of inquiry to facilitate critical and creative thinking at a level well beyond the possibilities of the traditional lecture.

Planning Framework

A good way to start the (re)design process is to reflect on a series of key questions about the course:

- What do you want your students to know when they have completed your blended learning course?
- What types of learning activities will you design that integrate face-to-face and online components?
- What means will you use to assess these integrated learning activities?
- How will information and communication technologies be used to support blended learning?

These and other key questions are outlined in Appendix Three: Redesign Guide for Blended Learning.

Next, discuss your responses to these design questions with an instructional design specialist and with other faculty, staff, and teaching assistants who are involved with the course. This discussion may also include instructional librarians and information technology (IT) personnel who are responsible for supporting the course. If you are redesigning an existing course you may also want to obtain present and past student feedback (surveys, interviews, focus groups) and input from faculty who teach related prerequisite or complementary courses. Offices of institutional analysis are also a good source for planning information. They often can provide student demographic data and success and withdrawal rates for specific courses and programs. Fink (2003) emphasizes the importance of using these data to "identify important situational factors that can inform the design of significant learning experiences for our students" (p. 68).

Based on the consolidation and interpretation of your planning data you are now in a position to construct the course outline or "blueprint" for your blended learning course. This is the document that will guide the design process and indicate to students the nature of inquiry and blended learning within the course. This outline should not only inform students about the learning outcomes, methods of assessment, and course policies, but should also clearly describe the reason for a blended learning approach and how it will be operationalized, the responsibilities of students, and the types of available support to help them succeed in the course. A template for preparing a blended learning course outline can be found in Appendix Nine, and a sample outline is in Appendix Ten.

For most students, blended learning will be a new experience; therefore, it is important to provide them with a proper orientation to the course. Our experience has shown that students who understand what the teacher plans for the course and why are in a much better position to engage positively in the learning activities and to achieve the course learning outcomes. On or before the first day of class, students should be introduced to the teacher, the course content, the course design, the reason for a blended design, and what is expected of them. Three items, in particular, must be addressed: a description and rationale for strategies of blended learning, structure and expectations for the course, and support and resources.

Description and Rationale for Strategies. A blended learning approach is selected because it is effective in supporting inquiry, reflection, and deep learning. Inform students if you are using a problem- or case-based approach, provide authentic questions, and explain that you expect them to engage in an inquiry approach. Share some of the literature about inquiry approaches and the effectiveness of blended learning. Provide students with an overview to deep, versus surface, approaches to learning (Ramsden, 2003) and effective teaching and learning ideas such as those described in "Seven Principles of Good Practice in Undergraduate Education" (Chickering & Gamson, 1987). Then discuss with the students how a deep approach to learning, as well as each of the principles of effective teaching and learning, have been incorporated into the design of the blended course. For example, longitudinal research studies from the University of Central Florida (Dziuban, Moskal, & Hartman, 2006) demonstrate that blended (or mixed-mode) courses have a higher student success rate than either face-to-face or fully on-line courses, and 86 percent of students followed in the study were satisfied or very satisfied with their blended courses, as opposed to only 4 percent who were unsatisfied or very unsatisfied. In addition, share comments from students who have previously experienced blended courses. For instance, students at the University of Wisconsin-Milwaukee (2002) state that blended courses provide increased flexibility and convenience with regard to time and learning location.

Course Structure and Expectations. The course structure—which may include face-to-face and online learning activities, expectations, and student responsibilities—must be clearly articulated. For example, when and for what objectives will the class meet in whole-group, face-to-face situations? When and for what reasons will small groups meet? What will be done individually? When and how will technology tools be used? What are the assignments and how will they be assessed?

Support and Resources. Explain to students the specific resources and software applications required and how they can access support. For instance, if a learning management system such as Blackboard or a Web-based conferencing system such as Elluminate Live! is used, direct students to the appropriate resources and support. For example, the e-Learning Web page at the University of Calgary (see http://elearn.ucalgary.ca/) is used to download instructional manuals and to view tutorials. For other software applications, refer your students to your institution's information technologies Web site. For example, see the Student Training site at http://www.ucalgary.ca/it/training/students.html. In addition, an institution's library may have many support options ranging from face-to-face sessions with instructional librarians to online tutorials and instruction. For example, see The Library Connection at http://library.ucalgary.ca/services/libraryconnection/. Students can also be directed to an online resource such as the *Workshop on the Information Search Process for Research* (WISPR) to help provide an inquiry framework for completing a major course assignment or project (http://library.ucalgary.ca/wispr/).

Student orientation to a blended learning course should be structured so that it supports (1) the social presence principle of developing a climate that will create a community of inquiry and (2) the cognitive presence principle of establishing critical reflection and discourse that will support systematic inquiry. In a blended environment, these two principles can be achieved by designing icebreaker learning activities that leverage the strengths of both face-to-face and asynchronous online communication. Icebreakers are fun activities that help support collaboration and the development of a learning community within a course (Dixon, Crooks, & Henry, 2006). For example, prior to the first day of class, an e-mail could be sent to students to indicate that a learning management system (LMS) Web site will be used to support the course and that they are required to log on to the site and complete an introductory survey. The focus may be to assess prior knowledge or experience students have with the course content or to discover why students are taking the class and what they hope to achieve with the experience. A discussion forum may ask the students to introduce themselves to the rest of the class to provide background information (such as where they are from) and query post-graduation activity. In addition, within the student Web pages section of a learning management system, such as Blackboard or WebCT, students could post a short biography and possibly a digital image of themselves. Icebreaker activities could then be designed for the first face-to-face session that capitalize on the information collected and shared on the course Web site.

Another variation would be to commence with a series of introductory activities within the first face-to-face class session. Begin by handing out copies of your course outline and reviewing the key points within a brief PowerPoint presentation. Students would then have ten to fifteen minutes to individually read the course outline and underline, highlight, or make notes about any questions, issues, or concerns. Next you could ask students to form small groups to discuss their questions and to try to help each other resolve them. Indicate that you will address questions they still have following their attempt to answer them in their small groups. Be sure to allow an appropriate amount of time for students to complete this process. Remind them that fellow students can often help them see things in a new light and suggest that they frequently discuss questions with other students. Suggest that they exchange names, phone numbers, and e-mails with several other students and then use these peers as a first line of support (for example, in sharing class notes, studying for tests, reviewing draft assignments).

This entire exercise could also be completed in a course Web site prior to or during the first week of the course. On an LMS Web site, you could post the course outline, create and post a narrated PowerPoint presentation with a tool such as Adobe Presenter to summarize the highlights of your outline, and set up small group discussion forums to facilitate student discussion and resolution of course-related questions, issues, or concerns. Questions that remain may be answered by the teacher during a face-to-face class session or in the main discussion area of the course Web site.

Several other introductory activities that may help orient students to a blended learning course include composing a digital letter or creating a narrated PowerPoint presentation to welcome students and briefly describe your teaching philosophy and the role you envision for students in the course. The digital letter can be e-mailed to students along with the course outline prior to the first class. Students on the first day of class may engage in an exercise to reflect on a very powerful personal learning experience, which may or may not have been school related. Have the students individually record their reflections and then form small groups to share their learning experiences and discuss why they were powerful. Debrief as a class about what makes learning experiences powerful, and relate the discussion to the blended teaching and learning approaches you envision for the course.

Facilitation Strategies

As noted previously, blended learning is framed by an inquiry approach to learning. Inquiry learning is problem or question–driven learning involving critical discourse, self–direction, research methods, and reflection throughout the learning experience. An inquiry approach supports and enriches the teaching, learning, and research process, and actively engages students in responsible learning activities. The practical inquiry described in Chapter 2 is used to frame the discussion of facilitation strategies. Within this model, inquiry is grounded in experience and integrates the public and private worlds of the learner within a community of inquiry. As previously outlined, this model consists of four categories or phases (see Table 7.1).

Blending learning should integrate campus and online educational experiences for the express purpose of enhancing the quality of the learning experience. Blended learning is an opportunity to fundamentally redesign the approach to teaching and learning so that higher education institutions may benefit from increased effectiveness, convenience, and efficiency. At the heart of blended learning redesign is the goal to engage students in

Table 7.1 Practical Inquiry Phases

Description	Category/Phase	Indicators
The extent to which learners are able to construct and confirm meaning through sustained reflection, discourse, and application within a critical community of inquiry.	Triggering event	Inciting curiosity and defining key questions or issues for investigation
	Exploration	Exchanging and exploring perspectives and information resources with other learners
	Integration	Connecting ideas through reflection
	Resolution/ application	Applying new ideas and/or defending solutions

Source: Garrison, Anderson, & Archer (2001).

critical discourse and reflection. The goal is to create dynamic and vital communities of inquiry where students take responsibility to construct meaning and confirm understanding through active participation in the inquiry process. These elements of blended learning have a profound influence on how we approach teaching and learning within higher education.

To assist in the rational selection and adaptation of particular strategies and tools, we described a classification of learning activities in Chapter Six. In particular, this classification identifies the dominant modes of communication associated with face-to-face and online learning. It also assists in understanding how the dominant modes of communication favor different cognitive activities. It should be noted that exploratory activities are more reflective, whereas confirmatory activities (integration, application) emphasize interaction and collaboration. The challenge is to integrate these activities so that their synergies contribute to a coherent and progressive educational experience.

An inquiry-through-blended-learning approach can be used to intentionally integrate these forms of communication to support the progression of inquiry through to resolution or application. This approach consists of four interconnected phases:

1. Before a face-to-face session
2. Face-to-face session
3. After a face-to-face session
4. Preparation for the next face-to-face session

Before a Face-to-Face Session

The first phase involves the use of communication technologies in advance of a face-to-face (F2F) session to "plant the seeds" for triggering events that will then be more thoroughly defined within the actual F2F session. Ausubel (1968) refers to these as "advance organizers" or anchoring events that provide entry points for connecting new information with the recall of prior, related learning

Table 7.2 Design Considerations Before a Face-to-Face Session

Nature of Inquiry	Learning Activities	e-Learning Tools/Resources
Learner	Reading/writing	Communication
Create a *triggering event*	Prereading assignment or activity on a specified topic or issue	Announcements section of a learning management system (i.e., Blackboard, WebCT)
Advance organizer		
Stimulate connections	Followed by a self-assessment quiz, survey, or discussion forum	Group e-mail feature within an LMS
Teacher		Posting or linking to prereading assignments
Determine learner's prior knowledge or experience with the topic or issue	Listening/writing	Web-based library indexes and abstracts
	Auditory/visual presentation of information	Social book marking (Delicious, Furl)
		Digital learning objects
	Followed by a self-assessment quiz, survey, or discussion forum activity	Podcasting
		Adobe Presenter
		Learning Object Repositories
		Self-assessment quizzes
		Test manager tools
		Anonymous surveys
		Survey tools
		Discussion forum
		Preclass discussion regarding questions and issue related to the required reading

experiences. There are a variety of learning activities and related e-learning tools and resources that can be used to support this phase. They include the use of Web-based readings with an accompanying online survey, quiz, or discussion form. This activity and several other examples are provided in Table 7.2.

The first priority is to establish communication with the learners so that they are clear about the rationale and expectations for the prereading assignments. This communication can be facilitated with a learning management system that allows the instructor to send a group e-mail to the class and post the corresponding information to the announcement section of the LMS.

Faculty have begun to also use digital audio and visual tools such as podcasting and Adobe Presenter to communicate with students before class time. Faculty can record short podcast information messages, which students are able to download and listen to, anywhere, anytime. Adobe Presenter can be used to narrate a lecture and embed self-assessment questions within PowerPoint presentations. Figure 7.1 shows a Presenter presentation where students can navigate in a nonlinear fashion by clicking on any topic. Advantages of these tools are that they allow students to listen and view course-related material outside of class time, at their own pace, and as often as required to gain understanding.

Figure 7.1 Adobe Presenter Example

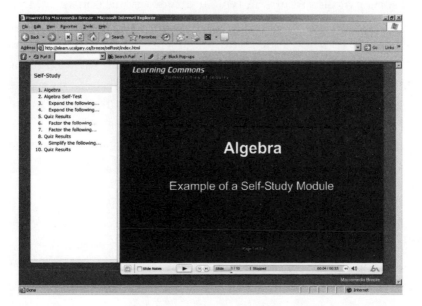

Faculty often require students to participate in a reading activity before a class session. Traditionally, this activity involved a reading from the course textbook. The option now is that students can be directed to a Web-based article or resource that is located within an online library database by using tools such as Proquest and Allectra. Some instructors also require students to find their own course-related articles and then post these resources to a social bookmarking system such as Del.icio.us (http://del.icio.us/) or Furl (http://www.furl.net/) so that all members of the class can access and comment on these Web sites.

A common challenge has been to meaningfully engage students in these preclass reading activities. Novak and colleagues (1999) have used the survey or quiz tool within an LMS to create triggering events for students in advance of a face-to-face class session. They have coined the term Just-in-Time Teaching (JiTT) to describe the process of getting students to read a textbook chapter or Web-based article and then respond to an online survey or quiz shortly before a class. The instructor then reviews the student submissions "just in time" to adjust the subsequent class session in order to address the students' needs, identified by the survey or quiz results. A typical survey or quiz consists of four content-based questions with the final question asking students: "What did you not understand about the required reading and what would you like me (the instructor) to focus on within the next face-to-face session?" An alternative to this activity would be to construct an online discussion forum to allow students to post questions or issues related to the preclass reading. This can be a powerful learning forum because students are able to read and respond to each other's questions in advance of the face-to-face session.

During a Face-to-Face Session

The second phase of the blended inquiry cycle involves the actual face-to-face session where learning technologies can be used to define the triggering event(s), provide opportunities for exploration, and create a first step toward the integration phase. This is probably the most significant aspect of blended learning course redesign. These face-to-face sessions are no longer used for information transmission such as lecturing but, instead, become opportunities to diagnose student misconceptions, foster critical dialogue, and support peer instruction. Table 7.3 outlines several in-class learning activities that can be supported with information and communication technologies. These activities are further described in the subsequent paragraphs.

If a survey, quiz, or online discussion forum has been used to support the preclass reading, the face-to-face session will often begin with a debriefing of this activity. Anonymous survey or quiz results can be projected (either by computer or with an overhead acetate printout) and reviewed by all students. The ensuing debate helps clearly define the triggering event and allows members of the class to begin sharing and comparing their perspectives and experiences related to the question or issue.

Web-based learning objects, such as interactive demand and supply curves for economic principles, can also be projected and discussed during class time to help students visualize and understand the relationships between key course concepts. These digital learning objects can often been found within repositories such as MERLOT (Multimedia Educational Repository for Learning Online Teaching—http://www.merlot.org/). Links to these objects can be made from the course LMS, thus allowing students to manipulate and review these learning resources after the class.

In larger classes, discussion and debate can be facilitated with classroom performance systems, commonly referred to as clickers. Crouch and Mazur (2001) suggest that these devices can be used to support a form of peer instruction. The process begins with the instructor posing a question or problem. The students initially work individually toward a solution and "vote" on what they believe is the correct answer by selecting a numbered or lettered response with their clicker. The results are then projected on a

Table 7.3 Design Considerations During a Face-to-Face Session

Nature of Inquiry	Learning Activities	e-Learning Tools/Resources
Defining the *triggering events* (key questions) Beginning to *explore* the questions	a) Talking/listening Dialogue with teacher and fellow learners about the specified issue or topic Mini-lecture and/or tutorial to address the results of the pre-class quiz or survey Large or small group discussion or activity Case study Initiation of an individual or group project	i) Displaying quiz or survey results LMS results for quizzes and surveys Overheads of information printed out from the LMS ii) Conducting in-class quizzes and surveys to promote dialogue and small- group work Classroom response systems (clickers) iii) Displaying digital learning objects and resources Objects uploaded to the course Web site and links to external learning object and resource sites (e.g., animations, video clips, PowerPoint presentations) Merlot (http://www.merlot.org/) iv) Displaying assignments and student work Assignment folders within LMS that contain the assignment handout, tutorial, resources, and examples of past student work

screen at the front of the room. A good question usually elicits a broad range of responses. Students are then required to compare and discuss their solutions with the person next to them in order to come to a consensus. Another vote is taken but this time only one clicker per group can be used. In most circumstances, the range of responses decreases and usually centers around the correct answer. A couple of alternatives to this process include having students generate the questions or use cell phones as the clicker devices.

Face-to-face sessions also present a good opportunity to initiate or clarify individual or group projects. To help students understand the expectations for these assignments, previous student work can be displayed and critiqued. Students can then either develop or use a preexisting assessment rubric to review the examples of past coursework. Similar to digital learning objects, these previous assignments can be uploaded or linked to the LMS so that students have access to the material after class time.

As class time is usually reduced in a blended learning course, we recommend that each of these face-to-face sessions conclude with a discussion to establish student responsibilities and action items for the online environment. This discussion can also be combined with a Web-based anonymous exit survey, which asks the students to state what they learned during the session and what they are still unclear about. This closing discussion and survey helps the students begin to integrate the new information received during the session with their prior learning experience. The survey data collected also provide valuable feedback for the instructor in terms of planning future face-to-face sessions and activities.

As indicated, transforming the focus of these face-to-face sessions from information dissemination (lecturing) to active and collaborative learning opportunities for students can be challenging. There are several additional resources that we recommend to help facilitate this process. For example, Kuh and associates (2005), in their book *Student Success in College:*

Creating Conditions that Matter, provide examples of effective practice for increasing levels of active and collaborative learning and student-faculty interaction within courses, programs, and institutions. Bean's (1996) book, *Engaging Ideas: The Professor's Guide to Integrating Writing, Critical Thinking, and Active Learning in the Classroom*, has an excellent section on designing tasks for active thinking and learning, and the book by Barkley and associates (2005), *Collaborative Learning Techniques: A Handbook for College Faculty*, outlines specific techniques that can be used to facilitate group work in face-to-face sessions.

Between Face-to-Face Sessions

The use of information and communications technology between the face-to-face sessions provides opportunities for the students to further explore and reflect on course-related activities. This phase begins with the use of the announcement board feature, within an LMS, to post a summary and a list of follow-up items from the face-to-face session. We recommended composing this announcement in a word processing document so that it can also be copied and pasted as a group e-mail message to the students. Table 7.4 presents an overview of how information and communication technologies can be used to support a series of reflective learning activities. We discuss each of these activities in this chapter.

As a communication tool, students can e-mail the instructor for individual questions or clarification of assignments, but we recommend that a "Frequently Asked Questions" online discussion forum be created within the LMS. Students can then share in the responsibility of answering questions and problem solving course-related issues. Online discussion forums can be used to promote individual reflection and critical dialogue between the face-to-face sessions. For example, a series of online discussion forums can be created by the instructor within an LMS, related to the key modules or topics for the course (Figure 7.2).

Table 7.4 Design Considerations After a Face-to-Face Session

Nature of Inquiry	Learning Activities	e-Learning Tools/Resources
Further exploration towards *tentative* *integration* with the ability to connect theory to practice application	a) Reading/writing	i) Anonymous surveys
	Anonymous class exit survey	Survey tools
	What did you learn from the class session?	ii) Communication
		Announcement section of your LMS site for student "to do" list
	What are you still unclear about?	Group e-mail feature for the student "to do" list
		Individual e-mail feature for individual student questions or clarification (try to put common questions into a Frequently Asked Questions discussion forum)
	Online discussion with student moderation	
	b) Talking/listening + reading/writing	Online discussion forums to facilitate student moderated discussions

(Continued)

Table 7.4 (Continued)

Nature of Inquiry	Learning Activities	e-Learning Tools/Resources
	Individual or group project work, case studies	Virtual classroom tools (Elluminate Live) for synchronous sharing sessions among student groups
	Preparation for next class:	iii) Individual and group project work
	a) Reading/writing	Assignment folders within LMS site that contain the assignment handout, tutorial, resources, and examples of past student work
	Preclass reading assignment or activity on a specified topic or issue	Group work area within an LMS that contains communication tools (e-mail, discussion forum, virtual chat) and a digital drop box for sharing documents
	Followed by a self-assessment quiz, survey, or discussion forum	Weblogs—reflective journaling tool
		Wikis—collaborative writing tools
		iv) Opportunities for further exploration
		External links section within LMS site for enrichment

Figure 7.2 Online Discussion Forum

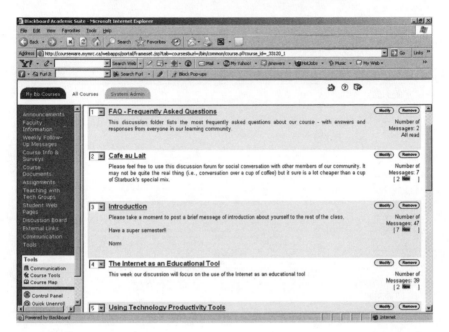

Groups of students (three to five) then select a module based on course readings, previous experience, interest in the topic, or all three. Each group is responsible for moderating and summarizing its selected online discussion for a set time (often one or two weeks). *Discussion as a Way of Teaching: Tools and Techniques for Democratic Classrooms*, by Brookfield and Preskill (2005), provides examples of the types of questions that can be used by students to create reflective discussion summaries or "discussion audits" (p. 72). These questions can be modified for online discussions. For example:

- What are the one or two most important ideas that emerged from this week's online discussion?
- What remains unresolved or contentious about this topic?
- What do you understand better as a result of this week's online discussion?

Figure 7.3 Wiki Online Discussion Summary

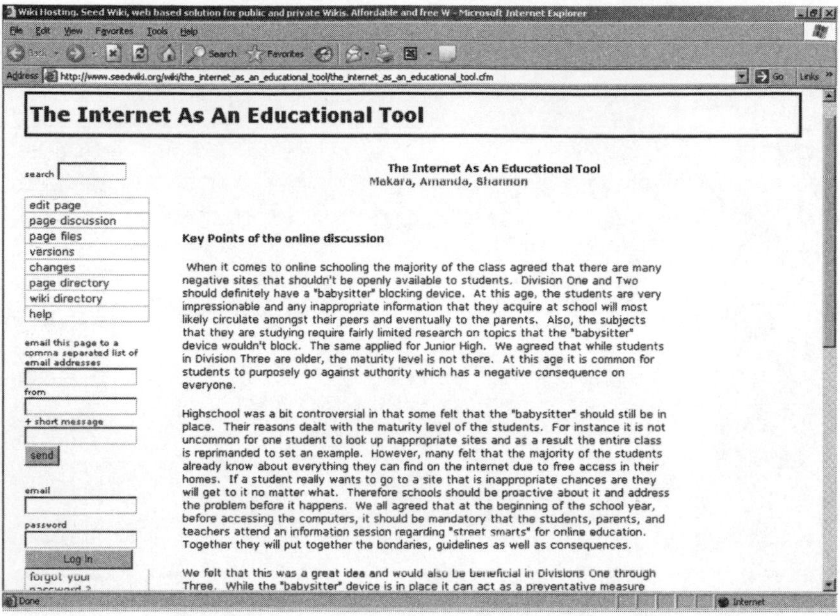

- What key word or concept best captures our discussion this week?
- What are some resources (e.g., Web sites, articles, books) that could be used to find further information/ideas about this topic?

A wiki (collaborative online writing tool) can be used to make draft notes and a final summary (synthesis and analysis) of the online discussion based on these questions or additional guidelines that are cocreated by the students and the course instructor (Figure 7.3).

Weblogs, a form of personal online journal, can be used to support self-reflection and peer review of course assignments (Figure 7.4). At the beginning of the semester, the instructor can require each student to create his or her own weblog. Examples are blogger.com or edublogs.org.

Figure 7.4 Weblog Reflection

Once an assignment has been completed and students have received assessment feedback, they then post responses to questions such as the following on their weblogs:

1. What did you learn in the process of completing this assignment?
2. How will you apply what you learned from this assignment to the next class assignment, other courses, or your career?

For weblogs to support peer review, students can attach drafts of specific course assignments to their blogs. Other students in the class can then either randomly or voluntarily select to review these documents and post responses to the author's weblog. Guiding questions for this peer review process could include:

1. What did you learn from reviewing this document?

2. What were the strengths (for example, content, writing style, format and structure) of the document?

3. What constructive advice or recommendations could you provide for improving the quality of this document?

Common complaints from students about group work is lack of time and difficulty in arranging meetings between the face-to-face sessions. The group tools within an LMS can be used to overcome this challenge. This tool set usually comprises a group discussion area, a file exchange system, e-mail links, and a synchronous chat feature. Students can use these tools to communicate and share files with other group members.

In addition, synchronous communication applications such as Elluminate Live! can be used to support student collaboration outside of the classroom. These applications allow students to participate in real-time online group meetings over the Internet. Within the meetings, students can use a whiteboard to brainstorm, a common browser to explore and review Web sites, and a shared desktop application that includes word processing, spreadsheet, and graphics software from one group member's computer to create and refine documents together. These sessions can also be recorded and archived for group members unable to attend a meeting.

Toward the end of this phase, another related inquiry-through-blended-learning cycle is introduced with a new learning activity such as the posting of a Web-based reading and survey or quiz. This activity should be designed to help students synthesize their learning from the current cycle and prepare for the subsequent face-to-face session.

Next Face-to-Face Session

In the next face-to-face session, information and communication technologies play a key role in helping complete an inquiry-through-blended-learning cycle or module by "closing the loop" between the online and face-to-face components of a blended

Table 7.5 Design Considerations for the Next Face-to-Face Session

Nature of Inquiry	Learning Activities	e-Learning Tools/Resources
Resolution/ Application	a) Talking/listening/writing Review of online discussion activities Individual or group presentations Final group thoughts on the topic or issue Initiation of dialogue on the next topic or issue	i) Display quiz or survey results LMS results for quizzes and surveys ii) Display of online discussion forum Online discussion forums within LMS iii) Display assignments and student work Assignment folders within LMS that contain the assignment handout, tutorial, resources, and examples of past student work

learning course. Table 7.5 describes the type of learning activities that can be used to help students achieve a sense of resolution or application to the course-related inquiry.

This process can be facilitated with a class discussion at the beginning of the face-to-face session. The inquiry phases of integration and tentative resolution are addressed by first reviewing the results of the anonymous exit survey from the last face-to-face session (Figure 7.5), and then discussing any student questions or concerns raised within this survey. If there was a class online discussion between the face-to-face sessions, the student moderators or the faculty member can provide an oral summary or some reflections about the discussion. Students can also be invited to demonstrate assignments in progress. These types of activities help clarify assignment expectations and consolidate student learning within the course.

Figure 7.5 Results from a Weekly Anonymous Class Survey

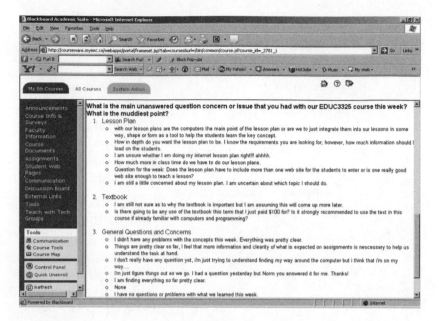

An inquiry-through-blended-learning cycle concludes with a brief wrap-up discussion, including final thoughts or comments, and then moves onto the next related question or topic, which in turn triggers the next related inquiry cycle.

Direct Instruction and Assessment

In Chapter Three we discussed the need for faculty to be more directive in their assignments in order to ensure that student inquiry progresses from exploration to application and resolution. We also indicated that assessment is at the core of any educational experience. The assessment process focuses student learning and presents the faculty member with opportunities to diagnose student misconceptions and direct students to relevant resources and support materials. This process should also give students the frameworks, guidance, and direction to become self-directed learners. In this section we offer examples of how

discussion forums, Web-based tools, classroom assessment strategies, and rubrics can be used to direct and assess student learning.

Discussion Forums

Discussions can be valuable forums where complex content and
perspectives are examined and understood through collaborative
processes and knowledge sharing. The discussions can take the
form of debates, small group work, and case studies. However,
if online discussions are incorporated into courses, there must be
consideration for whether and how to assess student participation
within these forums.

The teacher might first want to consider how important discussions are and what role they should have in the learning
experience—whether face-to-face or online. Most educators believe that to get the most out of a learning experience, students
must engage with course content and contribute to the class
discourse. One method of contributing ideas, knowledge, and
resources to the class is to participate in discussions.

If an online discussion is integral to your course objectives, you
should communicate an expectation for participation. Some faculty assign points to online discussion activities to help students
understand the importance of spending the time and effort to
contributing to, and learning from, discussions. Other educators
provide multiple and alternative methods for students to interact with content and perspectives, and allow students to choose
the activities they think will be of most benefit to them. This
allows for differences in both learning preferences and interests.
In either case, expectations need to be communicated.

Some educators set the general expectation that students will
participate regularly in online discussions and, with student input, they develop a scoring guide based on their own criteria for
quality work combined with student feedback. Students submit
a self-assessment of their discussion contributions with a grade
recommendation to the instructor to indicate how well they

believe they achieved the criteria indicated by the scoring guide. They may copy and paste actual examples of some of their postings to support their grade recommendation. The following three examples of assignments illustrate these concepts.

Example of Discussion Assignment and Scoring Guide. Students are required to read an article that offers multiple perspectives on a course-related concept. They then write a brief synopsis of the article to explain a perspective they support and why. This summary is posted to an online discussion forum. Students then read the postings of at least two other students and respond, respectfully, with further evidence from the article that supports or challenges the other students' interpretations. If someone receives a challenge to his or her summary, that student should be able to defend his or her position and refute the argument, or concede that the posting has compelled reconsideration of his or her original position. Table 7.6 demonstrates a scoring guide that can be used for this activity.

Self-Assessment. The number of postings is not a clear indicator of the quality and value of learning in online discussions. Therefore, students should be required to analyze and evaluate their own contributions, as well as what they have learned from reading and responding to the postings of other students. This is demonstrated with a reflection paper. Students are required to describe the extent to which they

- Posted messages to demonstrate critical analysis of course concepts
- Read and responded thoughtfully to the messages of others to support or challenge the content of the posts; asked critical questions or extended and elaborated their ideas
- Learned from others and changed or enhanced understanding

Table 7.6 A Scoring Guide for an Online Discussion Forum

Points	Competencies
4	Posts in discussions indicate careful reading of and critical reflection on reading assignments. Readily offers interpretations of course readings and supports opinions with evidence from the readings. Comments on other posts and responds appropriately to comments on own posts. Ideas are expressed clearly, concisely. Uses appropriate vocabulary. Is attentive to spelling and grammar.
3	Posts in discussions indicate reading and basic understanding of reading assignments. Supports some opinions with evidence from reading. Offers occasional comment on other posts and usually responds to comments on own posts. Ideas are sometimes unclear due to poor organization or poor word choice. Occasional spelling and grammatical errors.
2	Posts suggest incomplete reading or poor understanding of the material. Either does not offer an opinion on reading material or fails to support the opinion with evidence from the reading. Rarely comments on other posts and fails to respond to comments on own work. Frequent spelling and grammatical errors.
1	Posts are rare and do not answer the discussion question, or do not indicate reading and comprehension of the reading assignments. Does not comment on other posts or reply to comments on own posts. Spelling and grammar are so problematic that the message is garbled.
0	Student did not use the discussion board.

In order to complete this assignment, students are required to cut and paste examples from their postings to support their analysis. They are also asked to self-rate their participation as "outstanding," "good," "satisfactory," or "below expectations" and to suggest the grade they think appropriately reflects their contribution and learning within the online discussions.

Self-Coding. To help students become metacognitively aware of their online discussion forum contributions, assignments can be designed that require students to self-code their postings according to a particular framework, such as the practical inquiry model (see Figure 7.1).

This strategy can potentially increase students' awareness of their level of discourse within an online discussion and encourage them to think about how their responses relate to the course objectives. In addition, Pawan and associates (2003) suggest that faculty should provide direct instruction and model self-coding for this type of assignment. It may also be helpful for the educator to provide a metacognitive commentary for what he or she is doing and why. This could occur within the online discussion forum or with the use of a course weblog.

Voluntary discussion forums may also be included in which the level of participation and quality of postings are not assessed. Examples of this type of forum include social or café discussions in which students may make arrangements for social gatherings, share humor and event announcements, provide Q & A assistance for each other, or just "blow off steam" in a creative and supportive atmosphere. Or it may be decided that all students should contribute to a specific number of online discussion activities described in the assignment section of the course outline. A description of the criteria for satisfactory postings and responses, and the weight that each discussion will carry with respect to a course grade, is necessary. The discussions should be treated as any other assignment. The teacher or a teaching assistant will assign the marks.

Assign and structure the discussions with specific learning purposes in mind (and stated), and be clear about them with students. Ensure that it is indicated whether or not the discussion will be graded and what criteria will be used in the assessment process. Assess carefully the amount of time required for students to meet the discussion requirements and the amount of time required for the teacher to assess the quality of the work. Spend the time to construct creative, challenging, and engaging discussion assignments that promote critical discourse and reflection.

Web-Based Tools

To provide prompt feedback is one of the key principles in *Seven Principles for Good Practice in Undergraduate Education*, by Chickering and Gamson (1987). The authors state that reflection is critical to learning and that "knowing what you know/don't know focuses learning." Students require feedback on performance before, during, and after a learning experience.

In a study on course redesign, Twigg (2003) indicated that learning management systems, such as Blackboard and WebCT, can increase student opportunities for feedback and assessment, while decreasing the amount of time that faculty and teaching assistants spend preparing assessment activities, grading, recording, and posting results. Traditional assessment approaches in large introductory courses often involve only a midterm and final examination. But when a Web-based assessment tool is used, components of the assessment and feedback process can be automated to enable repetition and practice and frequent feedback. Research has consistently proven that repetition and feedback enhance learning. A Web-based tool can also significantly reduce faculty workload and increase free time for interaction with students.

Students can be regularly tested on assigned readings and homework with the use of online quizzes designed to probe their preparedness and conceptual understanding. These brief quizzes motivate students to keep current with the course material, as well as aid study structure and encourage more time spent on the task at hand. Using online quizzes encourages a "do it until you get it right" approach because students are allowed to take quizzes as many times as required to master the material. These types of online activities provide consistent, automated grading across sections and allow instant feedback for students when they are concentrating on the task.

Concept Reflection Assignment. Create three to four questions related to the key concepts of a prelecture reading assignment. One question could ask students to identify what they did not understand about the reading and what they would like covered in the lecture. An online quiz is then created from these questions. Prior to the lecture, administer the quiz, tabulate the results, and post them to the course Web site. Assign students a mark for completion of the online self-assessment quiz and then discuss the related quiz questions and issues in the lecture.

This assignment can also be modified by using a Web-based survey tool to gather student opinions or preferences regarding a particular topic, issue, or question before class. These tools can also be used to create a pool of self-assessment questions for student practice outside of class time.

Students can be involved in the assessment process by creating opportunities for them to develop their own review questions and to assess their peers' work. Be sure that assessment activities are congruent with the course learning outcomes and that these activities are designed to stimulate and assess critical thinking, not simply to recall information. For major assignments we recommend that the teacher or teaching assistants prepare individual student assessment reports rather than simply assign a grade in an online grade book. Not only does this personalize the assessment process, but also the qualitative comments contained within the report provide students with direct instruction for development and improvement of learning strategies in the course.

Classroom Assessment Techniques

Classroom assessment techniques are simple methods that educators can use to collect feedback, early and often, on how well their students are learning. The purpose of classroom assessment is to make sure that faculty and students have the information and insights needed to improve teaching effectiveness and quality of learning in a course. The feedback gleaned through classroom assessment can be used by faculty to adjust their teaching practices. Educators can also share feedback with students to help them improve learning strategies and study habits for more self-directed, metacognitively aware, and successful learning.

Educators who assume that their students are learning what they are trying to teach them are often faced with disappointing evidence to the contrary when they grade tests and term papers. Too often students have not learned as much or as well as was expected. There are gaps, sometimes considerable ones, between what is "taught" and what is learned. By the time faculty notice these gaps in knowledge or understanding, it is frequently too late to remedy the problems. Classroom assessment techniques (CATs) are instrumental to understanding what students are learning and which teaching strategies are effective in a particular course.

Traditionally, CAT activities have been administered at the beginning, middle, or end of a class period via paper and pen. However, this is very time consuming. From a student perspective, there is only a limited amount of time to properly reflect and respond to the activities. In contrast, faculty indicate that it takes a tremendous amount of time to collect, read, and collate the paper-based responses, especially for large classes. This is where Web-based assessment tools may be very beneficial. Web-based tools provide students with greater time flexibility to respond to the CAT activities and save faculty time by automating the collection and collation of the digital student responses. For example, a discussion board, quiz, or survey tool within a learning management system is ideal to create and post the CAT activity before or after a classroom session. Students can respond to the activity "anytime, anywhere" outside of the classroom. Faculty can "skim" the digitally collected feedback for trends and issues and then present and discuss the results during the following class session.

The Minute Paper. The Minute Paper is the single most commonly used classroom assessment technique. It provides a very simple way to collect written feedback on student learning. The technique is traditionally employed during the last few minutes of a class and requires students to respond to the following two questions on a sheet of paper or index card:

1. What was the most important thing you learned during this class?
2. What important question remains unanswered?

The survey tool within a learning management system automates this activity. The two questions can be used in an anonymous survey, and students can answer the questions outside of class time. A scan and trend of the responses is performed by cutting and pasting the text into a word processing document. The anonymous survey responses are then posted to the course site. The results are discussed with students during the next class session.

Other Examples. Before class, a background knowledge probe can be designed by creating two or three open-ended questions in a discussion board, a handful of short-answer questions with a survey tool, or a series of multiple choice questions with a quiz tool to assess students' existing knowledge of a particular concept, subject, or topic.

After class, using a discussion board, survey, or quiz tool, an expansion of the minute paper concept by students could allow them to comment on their "muddiest point" (least understood concept) regarding an online activity, such as a discussion forum, homework assignment, or video clip. An online discussion forum could also be used to support a "one-sentence summary" activity where students are asked to post one sentence to summarize a particular course topic. A variation of this activity is "What's the principle?" The instructor posts a problem to the discussion board and the students state the course-related principles that best apply to solve the problem.

Classroom assessment techniques should be used throughout a course to provide students with ongoing opportunities to reflect on their learning and for faculty to make informed adjustments to the course environment. The formative feedback collected from these activities should also be shared with the students to help them develop and shape their own learning strategies.

Assessment Rubrics for Student Assignments

A rubric is a scoring tool that lists the criteria for a piece of work or "what counts." Rubrics help illustrate course and assignment expectations and can save faculty valuable time during the student assessment process. Rubrics also aid educators and students in defining "quality" for a particular assignment. Generally rubrics specify the level of performance expected for several levels of quality. For example, a rubric for a paper or research project will list the items that a student must include in order to receive a certain score or rating. Rubrics also assist the students in understanding how their work will be assessed, as well as help them judge and revise their own work before handing in their assignments.

Andrade (2000) suggests that rubrics appeal to faculty and students for several reasons. First, they are powerful tools for both teaching and assessment. Rubrics monitor and improve student performance. Faculty expectations are clear and thus show students how to meet course expectations. The result is often marked improvement in the quality of student work and learning. Rubrics can also help students carefully judge the quality of their work and the work of their peers. When rubrics are used to guide self- and peer-assessment, students become increasingly able to spot and solve problems in their own and in one another's work. Also, rubrics can reduce the amount of time faculty spend evaluating student work. As an instructor, you may find that by the time an assignment has been self- and peer-assessed in accordance with a rubric, you have little left to say about it. If you do have a comment about an assignment, you can simply circle an item in the rubric, rather than struggle to explain the flaw or strength or terms for improvement. Finally, rubrics are easy to use and to explain. Montgomery (2002) states that with the use of rubrics in her courses, "students were able to articulate what they had learned" (p. 37).

Luft (1999) describes the challenges that have been identified with the use of rubrics to include the initial time required to create the rubric, the lack of clarification for assessment items, and the potential for the overarticulation of a task. These issues can be overcome with proper planning and design of the rubric. Table 7.7 provides an example of a rubric that could be used to assess student participation in an online discussion forum. An example for an e-portfolio assignment rubric is given in Appendix Eleven.

A rubric must provide a model for students. Examples of previous student assignments, with names removed, can be presented to demonstrate different levels of quality. A discussion forum can then be used to develop a list and corresponding criteria of what counts in quality work. Students can cocreate the assessment rubric with the teacher by articulating the gradations of quality, describing the lowest and highest levels of quality, and then filling in the middle levels based on their and the teacher's knowledge of common student problems.

A rubric is used to teach as well as to assess. All the terms used should be clearly defined, not be unnecessarily negative, and the terms and phrases should help students identify deficiencies to improve the next assignment. The use of rubrics can help students understand how their work will be assessed in a course. It is important that students are engaged in a discussion about the assessment rubric process so that they clearly understand what "quality" work means for a particular assignment.

Portfolios

There has been growing interest in the use of student portfolios as an assessment approach in higher education (Banta, 2003). Boyle

Table 7.7 A Rubric to Assess Participation in an Online Discussion Forum

Criteria	Level of Performance				
	0	1	2	3	4
Weekly discussion posting	Did not enter discussion	Poorly developed ideas; does not add to the discussion	Developing ideas	Well developed ideas	Well developed ideas (at least one full paragraph) and introduces new ideas
Discussion responses to instructor and other students	Did not enter discussion	Interacts once with either the instructor or other students	Interacts at least twice with instructor and/or other students	Interacts at least three times with instructor and/or other students	Interacts multiple times with instructor and/or other students
Evidence of critical thinking (application, analysis, synthesis, and evaluation)	Did not enter discussion	Poorly developed critical thinking	Beginnings of critical thinking	Some critical thinking evident	Clear evidence of critical thinking (application, analysis, synthesis, and evaluation)

(1994) summarizes this appeal in the following statement: "The portfolio, as an element of authentic assessment, has captured the interest of many instructors who want a more comprehensive way to assess their students' knowledge and skills, to have students actively participate in the evaluation process, and to simultaneously develop students' skills of reflective thinking. These latter features make portfolios an attractive alternative to traditional summative testing" (p. 10).

Most portfolios are used to communicate and present a range of student work over a period of time. Digital technologies can be used to support this process in the form of e-portfolios. Many of the strategies and tools that have been discussed in this chapter can be used within an e-portfolio framework. For example, Web-based authoring tools can be used by students to build and present their portfolios to a public audience. Weblogs can facilitate self-, peer, and instructor assessment through ongoing dialogue and reflection. Additional tools, such as wikis and video, can be used to create opportunities for students to communicate and document their learning through what Barrett (2004) refers to as a "digital storytelling for deep learning" process (p. 1). Paulson and Paulson (1996) suggest: "A portfolio tells a story. It is the story of knowing. Knowing about things . . . . Knowing oneself . . . . Knowing an audience . . . . Portfolios are students' own stories of what they know, why they believe they know it, and why others should be of the same opinion. A portfolio is opinion backed by fact . . . . Students prove what they know with samples of their work" (p. 2).

We recommend that teachers and students cocreate a rubric to assess the portfolio process such as the one highlighted in Appendix Eleven. In addition, the Assessment Reform Group (2002) emphasizes that the portfolio process should focus on assessment *for* learning: "Assessment for Learning is the process of seeking and interpreting evidence for use by learners and their teachers to decide where the learners are in their learning, where they need to go and how best to get there" (p. 1).

Conclusion

In this chapter we have provided a series of strategies and tools that can be used to guide and direct students in a blended learning course. These strategies and tools should not be incorporated as an "add-on" to an existing course. Instead, the course should be intentionally redesigned and planned so that these strategies and tools are used to meaningfully integrate face-to-face and online learning opportunities. During the first week of class, students should be given the opportunity to engage in a discussion with the instructor about the rationale and nature of blended learning. Faculty should use these strategies and tools to provide ongoing facilitation, monitoring, and modeling of the course expectations for students throughout the entire semester. Also, faculty should be prepared to offer more direction in their instructions and assignments so that students engage with their course work in a more focused and reflective manner.

We predict that increased adoption of the strategies and tools outlined in this chapter will lead to a significant shift in how faculty approach teaching and learning in higher education. In the final chapter, we identify emerging educational and technological developments that will drive blended approaches to teaching and learning and the future of higher education.

8

THE FUTURE

The context of higher education is changing. The convergence of social, technical, and intellectual forces has pushed higher education to the tipping point of a significant transformation. The forces of change have raised serious concerns about the quality of the educational experience in higher education. These realities will open the door to significant pedagogical redesigns that involve integrating conventional and innovative technologies. As a result, institutions of higher education are positioning themselves to adapt to the changing contextual realities.

The knowledge economy and ubiquitous communications technologies have precipitated significant societal changes and demands for new intellectual skills. Changing expectations of the quality of learning environments and outcomes has focused attention on preserving and enhancing the basic values of higher education while recognizing and adopting the enormous potential of Internet and communications technology. Blended learning is emerging as the organizing concept in transforming teaching and learning while preserving the core values of higher education. Our ability to capitalize on technological developments will most assuredly be founded on our understanding of a worthwhile educational experience.

Marshall McLuhan (1964) advised us that all new media are initially used to deliver the content of old media. This is certainly true of online learning, as the applications have been largely designed to make the traditional lecture more accessible. However, we are just now beginning to understand the strengths of new communications media and how they can address essential academic challenges in higher education. Access to information is not the challenge anymore. Creating and sustaining communities of inquiry is the new imperative—communities that stimulate and guide creative and critical reflection and discourse. Collaborative approaches to teaching and learning preserve the best of face-to-face learning and integrate that with asynchronous learning networks. New media have precipitated a contextual shift toward engaging students in deep and meaningful approaches to learning.

The Era of Engagement

Higher education is shifting from a passive teacher-centered approach to a transactional collaborative approach. Three forces of change have been largely responsible for this transformation.

The first profound change in higher education is the unprecedented advances in communications technology. In particular, the Internet has made possible a wide range of teaching and learning innovations associated with accessing educational opportunities and information. Online learning was the first step in this process of providing increased access and convenience to students. However, by itself, the Internet and online learning did not initially have the same transformative effect on higher education as it had in society generally. Approaches to teaching and learning were still dominated by information transmission techniques such as the lecture. Other forces were required to effect a transformation in teaching and learning.

The second set of changes is within the institutions themselves. There are budget constraints, an increasing focus on research, and growth in class sizes, resulting in a commensurate loss of contact with the professor. Efficiencies are needed to address the cost of higher education while addressing quality concerns. The challenge cannot be met by simply increasing funding for higher education. This is not a realistic prospect. Institutions of higher education have begun to recognize that they are in a difficult situation in terms of reducing costs while addressing quality concerns.

The third change is the recognition and the dissatisfaction with the quality of the learning experience in higher education. It is becoming clear to many, including students, that traditional methods are unable to address the need for higher-order learning experiences and outcomes demanded of a changing knowledge- and communication-based society.

The convergence of these forces of change has created the conditions under which it is imperative that higher education seriously consider new approaches to teaching and learning. As daunting as it may seem, these approaches must address financial constraints and quality concerns while maintaining and even enhancing the core values of higher education.

These forces are multiplicative and have converged to effect fundamental change. This convergence started to take shape at the beginning of the twenty-first century. Sustained educational discourse and collaboration came to the fore, and the visionaries recognized that it was not enough to simply layer these capabilities onto conventional delivery approaches to teaching and learning. Likewise, incremental changes will not address the challenges faced by higher education. Fundamentally new approaches and designs are required. The seeds for transforming higher education have been sown. Those seeds are blended approaches to learning.

Blended learning offers an approach and a way of thinking about the educational experience that avoids either/or choices and the downsides of online and face-to-face experiences. It offers a way to maximize effectiveness and efficiency. Online learning was perceived as isolating and did not fit well with the ethos of the campus-based higher education institution. Blended learning provided an acceptable means to question traditional face-to-face learning experiences in terms of not fully capitalizing on the opportunities of the Internet, or recognizing the potential of sustained online communities of inquiry. Alternatively, blended learning offers a way to extend and to enhance the educational experience in an effective and efficient manner.

As a result, blended learning has emerged as a major breakthrough to enhance both the quality of the teaching and learning transaction and the cost-effectiveness of designing blended learning courses. The early advocates, scholars, adopters, and senior administrators now are converging on a solution to the dilemma of addressing costs and enhancing learning. Most important, incentives are being put in place, and there is an increased adoption of blended designs by those in the mainstream of higher education. A critical mass of blended learning course designs serve as exemplars, having received the serious attention of leaders in higher education.

Blended approaches to learning are not just more trendy technology-driven ideas and gadgets that will fade as fast as they come. Blended learning questions conventional practices and the belief in the lecture as an effective approach to engage students in critical and creative thinking and learning. Blended learning designs illustrate how higher education can revisit and strengthen the fundamental values and practices that have been seriously compromised over the last half-century. Serious discourse about blended learning has reached the highest levels of academia.

From the students' perspective, rapid societal and technological changes have had a commensurate impact on how they think and learn. But it is not the talk of Net Geners, "digital natives," and Millennials, nor is it the suggestion that students want technology for technology's sake. In fact, it has been shown that higher education students are not totally swayed by technology and do have a discerning perspective about technology. Moreover, they appear to be more willing to challenge traditions. Certainly, undergraduate students have begun to question the quality of their educational experiences and are a major catalyst for change.

The coauthor of a recent study on students and technology stated that students "want to be linked in the network, but they want a lot of face-to-face time" (Kvavik, 2005). Moreover, students want this interaction not as an "extra" tagged onto the "normal" workload. To be purposeful and meaningful, such interaction must be integral to learning activities that allow reflection. Net Geners or Millennials are also much more predisposed to collaborative learning experiences (Dziuban, Moskal, & Hartman, 2006; Howe & Strauss, 2000). Students are knowledgeable about technology. They understand and want to use it when it makes sense and when it can enhance the collaborative learning experience. Changing student characteristics and expectations create the condition and reason for adopting blended approaches to course design. However, blended learning designs must get it right, and they must make sense to the demanding and critical Net Geners. Students want to be actively and collaboratively engaged in relevant learning experiences that have meaning and practical implications. In short, they want both face-to-face and online learning experiences that connect them to other students and the instructor. This represents a serious challenge for instructors and designers in meeting these expectations.

The forces cited above are flattening the educational world, not dissimilarly to the way the rest of society has been flattened (Friedman, 2005). Blended learning is about flattening the hierarchical control of the classroom with increased interaction and engagement. Students are being asked to assume increased responsibility for their learning but must be given commensurate control of the learning experience. Faculty are being encouraged to adopt new approaches, incorporate collaborative tasks, and develop technological skills. Institutions are being asked to provide attractive and welcoming common spaces for individual and collaborative inquiry. Classrooms will need to become more open, and learning spaces will need to become more flexible. Although for many this change is barely visible on the horizon, the transformation has begun.

The challenge is to reexamine the core values of higher education so that they will be enhanced and not lost. The goal is to create, enhance, and sustain the vitality of communities of inquiry. Higher education will be the poorer if the result is to simply deploy blended learning designs to find greater efficiencies but without the commensurate qualitative gains of purposeful collaboration. Frankly, higher education has to do better to improve the design, the facilitation, and the direction of meaningful learning experiences. There is no longer any reason to use the lecture to simply transmit information. Students can and should come to "class" armed with the most current information and be ready to engage in the critical and creative process of making sense of the information, followed by an exploration of the implications and applications.

Blended learning is the organic integration of thoughtfully selected and complementary face-to-face and online approaches and technologies. As a result, blended learning redesigns will multiply exponentially resulting in variations and related innovations that will spawn even further advances. The word *blended* is used to suggest that it is more than a bolting together of disparate technologies with no clear vision of the result. Blended approaches to educational design recombine concepts that were previously considered contradictory, such as collaborative-reflection and asynchronous-community. The primary measure of the impact of blended learning will be the qualitative shift in the process and outcomes of learning itself. The results will be most readily determined by the satisfaction of our students and the success of our graduates.

Tipping Point

Blended learning has been with us in various forms for some time. Only recently, however, has blended learning become an organizing concept and the focus of higher education. The idea of blended learning has spread quickly and with considerable resonance within higher education. It is becoming apparent to many that not only does blended learning have the potential to transform higher education, but it has already reached the "tipping point" in that transformation.

Insight into the impact of blended learning in higher education can be gained from Malcolm Gladwell's (2002) ideas about the spread of social epidemics described in his book *The Tipping Point*. Gladwell attempts to answer two questions: "Why is it that some ideas or behaviors or products start epidemics and others don't? And what can we do to deliberately start and control positive epidemics of our own?" (p. 14). Social epidemics "reframe the way we think about the world" (Gladwell, 2002, p. 257). Gladwell identifies three rules to answer the previous questions: the law of the few (messenger), the stickiness factor, and the power of context. We use these rules to demonstrate that blended learning has reached a pedagogical tipping point.

The Messenger

The first rule speaks to those who incubate and promote the social epidemic. Gladwell (2002) states that "the success of any kind of social epidemic is heavily dependent on the involvement of people with a particular and rare set of social gifts" (p. 33). In the case of blended learning, we can identify a few insightful and passionate individuals and scholars who recognized its transformative potential and were able to communicate and demonstrate its power. One of these individuals is Carol Twigg (2003), the leader of the Pew course redesign project and advocate for the fundamental redesign of large enrollment courses in higher education, a person who revealed to many in higher education the effectiveness and the efficiencies gained with a commitment to fundamentally rethinking course redesign.

Since blended learning has been with us in various forms and contexts for awhile, what has caused blended learning to become so contagious now? Why does the idea suddenly make sense to those beyond the early adopter? First, the concept is simple and intuitively appealing—notwithstanding its complexity in application. Second, blended learning is adaptable so that each professor can customize the approach to his or her needs. Third, there is little risk in terms of values and reputation. The mainstream has recognized that a blended approach is in their, and their students', best interests. Finally, initiatives such as those of the Pew course redesign project provided exemplars that revealed the possibilities and gave implicit permission to test a blended approach. This takes us back to the scholars, visionaries, and connectors who communicated the idea that resonated with those in the mainstream. If respected teachers redesign their courses, this will give permission to others to be more open and not fear being regarded as odd or as putting students at risk.

Stickiness

Blended learning has "stuck" because it is a means to change but also a means to stay the same through preserving long-held values and beliefs about higher education. Blended learning is infectious in the way it actually preserves and enhances the ideals and ethos of higher education. As appealing as this may be to many in higher education, it is not sufficient. A rigorous plan is required that is sustainable and has incentives—this is the main "stickiness factor." Incentives are powerful motivators in any organization or business. This is particularly so in higher education because professors are essentially independent contractors and are not greatly influenced by the power of senior administrators or the bureaucracy.

Blended learning is inherently sticky as well because of the blend of the real and virtual worlds. Integrating these elements is critically important for "stickiness." The clarity of purpose associated with face-to-face and online communities that are complementary is a crucial design and stickiness factor. Blended learning holds learners' attention for the right reasons—reflection and discourse. Stickiness is meaningful engagement on a topic of interest directly related to the purpose of the course. Online learning focuses attention on the ideas and the construction of new concepts and knowledge structures. The challenge to maintaining stickiness is to sustain reflection and discourse through the full integration of real and virtual communities.

Context

It is this unity of the public (collaborative) and private (reflective) worlds that makes the context of blended learning unique. The challenge is to design the context of blended learning to approach the full potential of blending collaborative and reflective learning. The power of the context of blended learning is that it also facilitates the development of personal exchanges that can be sustained beyond the course and over time. The online context eliminates the barrier of memory. It allows the participant to manage more information and better communicate complex ideas. It also allows each participant to invest more time and interaction in their learning. The context of a well-designed blended learning experience can have a dramatic effect on the participants and the learning outcomes.

Context is powerful in education. It shapes whether students approach learning in a deep and meaningful manner or in a surface and expedient manner. The reason for the power of context is the control of the teacher as designer and facilitator. The context of blended learning offers students the opportunity to convey their thoughts in a context free of anxiety and to receive feedback free of ridicule. Face-to-face environments build personal bonds that then allow participants to continue to be engaged online. One is connected yet free to conceive, construct, and compose one's thoughts, thoughts that can then be shared and nurtured for further growth. Online learning provides opportunities for critical discourse without the obligation to necessarily conform, which sometimes happens in a face-to-face context. In a blended learning context, freedom of thought and expression does not mean isolation. Engagement is stimulated as much by other members of the community as it is by the teacher. Each participant provides teaching presence. Within the structure of the design and the influence of a leader, responsibility for learning is shared among all participants. Learning activities are shaped, enhanced, and extended through collaboration in a blended community.

In summary, we are on the cusp of a contagion. Blended learning has become contagious because it addresses the quality of the educational experience in higher education as well as the use of technology to enhance the ideals of traditional higher education. We have reached the tipping point where blended learning will transform higher education. Scenarios we have provided resonate with faculty and are being shared in an exponential manner. Blended learning has been infectious because the timing is right, and it is very hard to discount its intuitive appeal and ability to address pressing issues.

Final Thoughts

We have provided the rationale for why we believe blended learning will transform teaching and learning in higher education. Blended learning is a commonsense, pragmatic approach to redesigning teaching and learning in higher education. Blended learning will transform teaching and learning in fundamental ways. However, transformation is not a revolution. Higher education is experiencing an evolutionary transformation. Numerous converging events brought us to this point. For example, higher education has struggled with the expansion of enrollment since the 1950s. Internet and communication technologies have transformed society since the 1990s, but the same cannot be said for higher education. Funding for higher education has put much of higher education on a starvation diet. As a result, current methods are being seriously questioned from an effectiveness and efficiency perspective. Finally, as dissatisfaction increases, the concept and practice of blended learning reaches the tipping point. Blended learning is both a catalyst and a solution for the challenges of effectiveness and efficiency that have emerged at a time that thinkers in higher education are open to change and searching for solutions.

Blended learning addresses the issue of quality of teaching and learning. It is an opportunity to address pressing pedagogical concerns, while distinguishing and enhancing the reputation of institutions of higher education as innovative and quality learning institutions. The focus has shifted to learning itself. Convenience and efficiencies are acceptable goals as long as there are commensurate increases in the quality of the learning experience. The fusion of online and face-to-face approaches will see a great release of design and learning energy and innovation. Without investment in the exploration and redesign of teaching and learning that integrates the best of face-to-face and online learning, we put higher education institutions at a competitive disadvantage. The risk is now entirely on the side of inaction.

Blended learning is not about technology. Campus-based institutions' interest in e-learning is dissipating, which clearly reveals that faculty are not interested in adopting technology for technology's sake (European ODL Liaison Committee, 2004). Students are open but skeptical to technology in the classroom. They want to see it used in educationally appropriate ways—not just for its own sake. Students are beginning to assert that it is not acceptable to be deprived of interaction with their professor, that the course content is irrelevant, the tasks are trivial, outcomes are meaningless and of little value, and expectations and workload are unreasonable. Student dissatisfaction has become a serious problem, and the reputation and recruitment of institutions are at risk. Faculty must open their classrooms to discourse and encourage collaboration among students. Senior administrators have begun to recognize blended learning as the most viable means to address this challenge with finite resources. Higher education is not going to be transformed once and for all. It will not settle back to a steady state. The new era in higher education is a continuous and progressive state of transformation.

Curriculum will continue to be organized around courses. However, the structure of the educational process itself will be flexibly coupled in terms of face-to-face and online elements. What will be different is the flexibility and adaptability of the learning process. The greatest change will occur with the ability to engage students in reflective discourse and the ability to adjust to the learner's individual and collaborative needs. In short, change will occur with the ability to create and sustain a community of inquiry. Large lectures are being recognized as ineffective from a meaningful learning perspective. Blended learning offers the opportunity for higher education to catch up with the communications revolution. Continuous connectivity provides authentic collaborative learning experiences congruent with the development of critical and creative thinkers in a rapidly evolving knowledge society.

The shift to more flexible and interactive educational environments will have an enormous effect on how institutions define and brand themselves. This is crucial because these changes will bring increased competition in higher education for the best and brightest faculty and students. Institutions have to distinguish themselves from the competition. To do this they must continue to adapt and invest in teaching and learning innovation and support. Blended approaches to teaching and learning will become a recruiting advantage. For students and faculty, blended learning will be seen as an effective and efficient way to learn and teach while meeting other personal and professional goals. Students will have more time to interact with their fellow students and gain work experience. Faculty will have more time to spend with their students, as well as on their research.

Blended learning is an important and timely approach to teaching and learning in higher education. When combined with the community of inquiry framework, blended learning can provide a means to rethink how we can improve teaching and learning in a cost effective manner. Notwithstanding the transformative effects of blended learning, there will come a time when the blended learning distinction will dissolve as a useful label. The reason is that all learning will be blended to some degree. Blended learning will just be the way learning occurs. In the meantime, however, the concept of blended learning is a rallying call and a powerful concept to mobilize innovation to address the real challenges of engagement and access in higher education.

Appendix 1

ORGANIZATIONAL CHANGE

There have been a number of reports that document the disruption of higher education as a result of new and emerging communication and Internet technologies. Typically, the reports reveal that the "impact of information technology will likely be profound, rapid, and discontinuous" (*Preparing for the Revolution*, 2002). According to Frost and Chopp (2004), higher education is facing pressures and challenges on numerous fronts—attracting students, top scholars, and funding. What also stands out is the challenge to secure great leaders as the rate of turnover increases. It is becoming very clear that for higher education to meet these challenges, it must develop a "capacity to adapt and change as new modes of knowledge formation emerge" (Frost & Chopp, 2004, p. 46). The two core ingredients in this transformation of knowledge formation in higher education are leadership and technology.

Unlike most other large organizations, technology has had relatively little impact on higher education. The case is made by Duderstadt, Atkins, and Van Houweling (2002), who state, "To date, the university stands apart, almost uniquely in its determination to moor itself to past traditions and practices" (p. 18). The authors point out the limited, marginal use of learning technologies and then note the irony "that the very institutions that played such a profound role in developing the digital technology now shaping our world are the most resistant to reshaping their activities to enable its effective use" (p. 18).

As proposed throughout this book, there must be a shift in how we approach teaching and learning. We need an approach that recognizes the technological advances facing graduates, an approach that uses those same technologies to prepare graduates to be the critical and creative thinkers that are essential in the knowledge era. The appropriate and thoughtful adoption of technological solutions will most assuredly demand creative leadership. The alternative is to live in the past or "react and lurch about, motivated by fear of being left behind" (Collins, 2001, p. 162). To date, we see more "lurching about" than we do transformational leadership. Although this may seem somewhat harsh, new ways of thinking and great leadership are much in demand for higher education to set itself on a course of purposeful and sustained change.

Changing Leadership Approaches

To date, innovation in higher education has consisted largely of random add-ons. These so-called "innovations" are too often overhyped technological gadgets that dazzle but do not address sound pedagogical issues and detract from fundamental goals—particularly regarding the benefits of communication and Internet technologies, which are much discussed but have marginal impact at best on the learning experience. Typically, the technology is used to access ever more information, which results in further overloading students and providing less opportunity to think deeply and to truly understand. Another limited approach is to add a discussion board that is not integral to the lesson. Voluntary participation is then short-lived. Such capricious and unsystematic tactics do little to enhance the quality of the learning experience and simply mean more work with little benefit. The only consistent outcome is that of further taxing limited resources.

We argue here that the scarcity of fundamental change in the higher education classroom stems not from a lack of resources but from a lack of understanding of what is possible by thoughtfully blending traditional face-to-face approaches with online learning. Although it may be clear to most that current practices are not sustainable, we must do more to position ourselves for the future. We must avoid busying ourselves by spending enormous amounts of time revising obsolescent approaches and practices. If we are not willing to stop ineffective practices, lack of resources will continue to be the scapegoat and nothing will change.

The hope for higher education is in attracting great leaders. Certainly higher education will not be able to buy its way out of its situation. Transformation must be driven by the need and demand for higher-quality learning experiences. Expensive add-ons will not address the quality challenge. New ways of thinking and great leadership are the ways to fundamental change. What are those leadership characteristics and attributes required to cope with the changing societal expectations of higher education, quality challenges, and technological advances?

Leadership Characteristics

The view of leadership during the last century was that of a charismatic individual who could publicly represent the organization well. However, in light of the recent corporate scandals, many are beginning to seriously question these characteristics as being sufficient for successful leadership of complex organizations. The challenges of leadership today demand abilities that go well beyond an individual with an engaging personality who can provide good sound bites and has an uncanny knack of remembering names. Leadership today requires a more substantive knowledge of the nature of the business and a commitment to facilitate the success of the organization. It is this insight that is crucial if an organization is to remain vital, dynamic, and focused. This is no less true of higher education.

Three core elements or interrelated sets of characteristics—vision, interpersonal skills, and courage—constitute leadership

(Garrison, 2004). The first characteristic of true leadership is vision and insight. A vision of the future requires first-hand knowledge and insight into the needs of clients, challenges, and the fundamental values and ethos of the institution. A leader must also be open to refine this vision and to facilitate collaboration through critical engagement with internal and external stakeholders. Vision must be credible in the sense that it is in the best interests of the institution as a whole and is truly shared. Achieving this requires a second set of abilities.

The second set of successful leader characteristics is the interpersonal skills needed to work collaboratively with others. The most recognized skill is that of communication. However, communication does not consist only of rhetorical skills but also the ability to listen and share—that is, to learn. In this regard, the ability is a corollary of vision in that communication is essential to having a shared vision and to continually map new directions. Successful leaders are not afraid to share their ideas and are willing to listen to contrary views. A less obvious characteristic of a great leader is one who can recognize talent and be able to position that talent to make the greatest contribution for the organization. Collins (2001) argues that in the hierarchy of leadership, executive leadership (highest level) has the ability to get the right people on board. Great leaders decide who is the best person, concurrent with deciding on the best course of action. Leaders must tap into the very best intellectual resources and deploy such people in areas and ways that match their competencies and interests. Conversely, they must have the courage to recognize where there is little or hostile talent, and be prepared to remove or neutralize the impact of these individuals. Finally, great leaders are quietly committed to the task of making the institution a success and willing to be held accountable. There is a growing intolerance in institutions for flamboyance and bravado.

The third characteristic, and one that is least in evidence in higher education, is courage. Courage is the willingness to strive for an ideal and a purpose greater than oneself. Substantive change must begin with a serious questioning of existing practices. The evidence of great leadership is in action, not rhetoric. Today, leaders must be intimately connected to action and be able to work closely with the change agents. Opportunities must be seized and change expedited. It takes courage to make necessary but difficult decisions. Difficult decisions will most certainly mean discontinuing certain programs and practices. This may be the most difficult lesson for those in higher education to accept. Leaders must have the character to do the right thing but also to be able to work with people and treat them fairly. Not unlike teaching, a successful leader must be both facilitative and directive. Without the commitment to implement change with a focus on results, vision and personal attributes are for naught.

Much can be learned about leadership by reflecting on the intersection of the three constituent elements of great leaders. When vision and personal attributes intersect, we see a manifestation of good judgment and integrity. It is the ability to see what needs to be done and the personal integrity to advocate for and defend one's beliefs and vision. At the intersection of personal attributes and courage is authenticity; that is, to have the courage to be open and respectful of others, including listening and learning from contrary arguments. Finally, when vision and courage intersect we witness a commitment to change and willingness to put one's reputation on the line. Great leaders lead from the front and are accountable for their decisions.

Leadership is about ideals and ideas combined with the character and courage to precipitate real change. All the high-minded talk of leadership means nothing without the courage to make decisions in a timely manner to produce results. Results are seldom as expected, but remain the only way for continued progress. Leadership is about making the necessary corrections based on an objective assessment of previous decisions.

In the final analysis, we need to reflect upon the type of leadership appropriate for the challenges we face as we move into the twenty-first century. Admittedly, strong and effective leadership is complex and seemingly contradictory. It requires an exceptional person to be a visionary who is sufficiently down-to-earth to design and implement action plans, to have the ability to listen but also know when to be decisive, to be flexible but firm in implementing change, to be demanding but compassionate, to move forward confidently but be ready and willing to recognize inevitable missteps, and, finally, to be accountable for results.

Leadership and Instructional Approaches

As discussed at the outset, leadership is a pressing necessity in higher education as a result of increasing expectations, reduced funding, and the pervasive impact of communication and Internet technology. Although transformational leadership is required to enhance quality on several fronts, the area of highest priority is the quality of teaching and learning. Courses need fundamental redesign to address serious classroom limitations associated with consistently achieving quality learning outcomes such as critical thinking and self-directed learners. The traditional classroom model is seriously challenged by those dissatisfied with large lectures as the main higher education learning experience. Students are beginning to insist on a more active involvement in relevant learning tasks. Some institutions of higher education will be receptive and gain a competitive advantage with the redesign of the learning experience and the appropriate use of communication and Internet technologies. In this regard, there will be winners and losers in an increasingly competitive higher education field.

Higher education is an international enterprise. The very best leaders, faculty, and students are mobile. Universities are in a globally competitive race but have shown little awareness of this challenge. To date, students have survived in spite of the system. The question is how much longer will higher education students, and society, accept passive and seemingly irrelevant information transfer with few opportunities to hone critical thinking and problem solving skills?

Online learning has enormous potential to shift the way we approach teaching and learning in the support of higher-order learning (Garrison & Anderson, 2003). Online learning adopts the capabilities of new and emerging Internet communication and information technologies to enhance and expand the ability to create communities of inquiry that facilitate critical discourse and meaningful learning experiences in a convenient and cost-effective manner. With a reconceptualization of teaching and learning, it is possible to capitalize on the asynchronous communication and conferencing capabilities of online learning and provide the connectivity and reflective freedom essential for critical and creative thinking and learning (that is, connective asynchronicity). Online learning offers the ability to be part of a dynamic and sustained community of learners engaged in critical discourse and reflection with the express purpose to construct meaning and confirm knowledge (Garrison & Anderson, 2003).

Connective asynchronicity, however, in most situations, is not the complete answer to enhance the quality of the learning experience in higher education. Online learning cannot easily replace the advantages and the need of learners to connect verbally in real time and in contiguous space. For this reason, online learning is increasingly being conceived as in partnership with face-to-face classroom learning experiences. This blending of classroom and online learning offers a rich and full array of communication options that range from spontaneous, free flowing verbal exchanges to reflective, well-defined written exchanges. However, blended learning is more than an enhancement of either online learning or the classroom learning experience. Blended learning takes advantage of the integration of verbal, written, and visual communication to support and facilitate interactive and reflective higher-order learning.

The potential of blended learning is found in its congruence with the traditions and values of higher education. There is a growing recognition that blended learning can address funding shortfalls and preserve and enhance the ideals of higher education (Twigg, 2003). Blended learning precipitates rethinking teaching and learning approaches in higher education. It invites faculty to (re)design learning experiences. Learning experiences can be designed that are best suited to spontaneous verbal discourse and reflective written communication. If the intention of higher education is to facilitate critical thinking and higher-order learning, leaders must start the planning and the positioning of their institutions to adopt blended approaches to learning that create sustained communities of inquiry—the hallmark of higher education (Garrison & Kanuka, 2004).

Institutional Change Scenario

An awareness of the potential for blended learning as a catalyst for change is emerging in higher education. However, much needs to be done at the institutional level to raise awareness and understanding of the potential for blended learning. In this regard, it is essential that institutions provide credible speakers to describe blended learning. Senior administration must be supportive partners in this process of raising awareness. Concurrent with this process, the drafting of position papers and policy documents must be initiated.

Sound policy is required if higher education is to avoid capricious and opportunistic developments, wasted resources, and continued classroom deficiencies. For change to occur in a desirable and systematic manner, clear policy principles and strategic plans are essential. In this regard, we must be able to publicly ask policy questions, debate issues, and articulate a defensible rationale. Why should higher education adopt blended learning approaches? What is the nature of the educational experience that blended learning represents? How does blended learning challenge traditional assumptions and practices? How will blended learning change expectations for faculty and students? How will the adoption of blended learning be managed?

Policies are needed that reflect institutional values, principles, and direction. Blended learning must be shown to be consistent with the values of the institution and be able to enhance institutional goals. Policy documents provide the rationale necessary to gain the support for change. If blended learning, and the transformation of teaching and learning, is the goal, then blended learning must be clearly articulated and linked to other institutional policy documents. In this way, policy can map out strategic direction, set priorities, and allocate resources.

A policy framework should provide a vision, guiding principles, a rationale, challenges, goals, initiatives, incentives, and outcomes. Policy presents a case for change and sets direction. It is the conceptual framework for strategic action plans that consider specific initiatives, roles, infrastructure, resources, professional development, assessment, and accountability measures. Although the process for policy development can provide the means for acceptance and set direction, only an inert document will be produced without collaborative leadership and institutional commitment in the form of incentives. Senior administrative officers must be clearly supportive by articulating a vision statement and being prepared to commit resources. In addition, senior administration must facilitate collaborative leadership by bringing together leaders from across all levels of the institution. No one leader can facilitate transformational change.

A lesson can be learned from the University of Central Florida's sustained faculty development support programs. To "achieve consistency, quality, and scalability," they state, "it is necessary to establish a central service coordination unit with sufficient resources to develop and apply standards and support the expanding volume of work that will result from increased faculty demand" (Hartman & Truman-Davis, 2001, p. 55). Redesign support is essential to ensure early successes and provide prototypes that will help others understand the benefits and possibilities.

The key strategic principles of leadership and support are demonstrated in the following scenario of a midsized research university challenged by quality and access demands. Other issues and challenges such as standards, copyright, merit and promotion, communication, infrastructure, assessment, and accountability are also identified.

Our scenario for change is that of a commuter research university with 30,000 students. It is located in a fast-growing city of over one million people, and it cannot meet the rapidly increasing enrollment demand of qualified students. There is a severe shortage of space and a concern with student satisfaction of the learning experience. The university has a very good research reputation and has received significant research investment. The teaching and learning investment, however, has not been matched. Students and the larger community have begun to question the quality and investment at the undergraduate level.

Some time ago the university embarked on a major curriculum redesign project. The goal was to redesign curriculum for higher-order learning outcomes such as critical and creative thinking. In 2002, the university realized that it needed to focus on process issues and so adopted inquiry-based learning as the defining feature of the university's approach to teaching and learning. Concurrently, it was acknowledged that true inquiry approaches could not be realized without capitalizing on the potential of communications and information technologies. Up to this point, the campus-based university had not given much institutional attention to learning technologies.

The provost recognized the need for an institutional learning plan if it was to elevate the importance of teaching and learning and mobilize support for innovation. The Academic Program Committee, a core academic governance committee, charged a subgroup of faculty to write an institutional learning plan. The learning plan was to be a companion document to the university's academic plan. The Boyer Commission (2001) provided the inspiration for inquiry approaches in higher education. The learning plan outlined the principles, guidelines, rationale, action items, and progress measures. This document provided the rationale for learning technology and identified specific recommendations. It identified blended learning as a design approach that was consistent with the values and mandate of the university.

Immediately following the draft of the learning plan, the same subcommittee was tasked with the responsibility to develop a blended learning position paper. Beyond the integration of face-to-face and online learning, blended learning would be a process to restructure traditional class contact hours—a means to rethink and redesign conventional approaches to teaching and learning that were increasingly reliant on the lecture. A list of policy issues and an action analysis was provided. Financial support, design support, technology infrastructure, copyright, intellectual property, and recognition were identified concerns needing resolution. Finally, although the potential for both effectiveness and efficiency gains were noted, it was clear that the subcommittee felt the university should focus primarily on effectiveness and the enhancement of the quality of the learning experience.

The blended learning position paper was shared with deans and department heads. Focused discussions were conducted to identify the need for a position paper and how it could address growing concerns of space utilization and student satisfaction. The issue of blended learning continued to be raised in a variety of public forums by the provost. From the individual faculty member's perspective, it was clear that faculty support for blended learning redesign would only be possible if faculty could be assured that blended learning could (1) enhance inquiry learning experiences, and (2) offer efficiencies to faculty in terms of their teaching responsibilities. These assurances provided a direct link to the academic and learning plans and offered advantages to the individual professor. It was determined that to ask faculty to redesign their courses for administrative efficiencies, cost savings, and access would be a very hard sell. The university enrollment was already over capacity, and faculty had shouldered the burden of cutbacks for nearly a decade.

As university leaders were brought on board, a broader communications strategy emerged. Once the reasons for blended learning were made clear and were found agreeable, a variety of messages and media were used to raise awareness. A Web site was created, information handouts were produced, articles were written for the university newsletter, workshops and seminars were offered, and high-profile speakers were brought to the institution. One event proved to be a turning point. This was an invitational seminar for senior members of higher education institutions and government officials. Extensive discussions followed the keynote address, and considerable enthusiasm and support was evident. The final breakthrough came when the president raised the profile of blended learning by including it in various communiqués and identifying it as a budget priority.

In two years of the blended learning initiative, real resources were targeted to course redesign. An inquiry and blended learning course redesign project was established and $200,000 was provided. Request for proposals were sent out and a competitive vetting process established. Thirteen projects were supported in the first round. Each of the projects was given $10,000 for course release and multimedia development. The remaining funds were used to assist with development support. This program was repeated in the second year with another eleven projects funded. One of the projects received $30,000 to redesign a large-enrollment class. The success of this pilot program gave senior administration the confidence to create a high-level committee to oversee it and to invest in this program on a continuing basis.

A special redesign support course called Inquiry Through Blended Learning (ITBL) was established to provide continued faculty development for the projects. Although the primary focus for ITBL was design support for blended learning, it was framed from an inquiry perspective to allow faculty to view redesign from an educational perspective in contrast to seeing blended learning as only a technological innovation.

ITBL attendance was required of the project leaders, but with a flexible approach. The intent was to model blended learning and have faculty experience it as they struggled to redesign their courses. The cohort would meet once a month to share their thoughts, resolve challenges, and receive instruction. Project teams kept in touch between sessions with online communication in an attempt to create a sustained community of inquiry. Special seminars and workshops were offered and considerable individual consultation was provided. Members of the ITBL instructional design team met with each of the project teams before the first face-to-face ITBL session and continued to schedule meetings as required. This helped develop confidence in the redesign approach, as well as ensure that transformative redesign was achieved. There was no particular end date to ITBL, other than the implementation of the design. Even at that point it was hoped that project leaders would remain part of the ITBL community and assist the new project leaders with their experience.

Emphasis was also placed on assessing the impact of the redesign efforts. It was essential that the university learn from these efforts to ensure the success of future redesigns. It was equally important to provide data to convince senior leaders and faculty that ongoing investment was worthwhile. To this end, evaluation data were gathered on all course redesigns. Data were gathered from faculty with regard to successes, challenges, support, and what they would do differently. Student evaluation data included why they selected a blended course, amount and quality of the interaction, course design and expectations, most and least effective aspect of the course, and overall satisfaction. These results were combined with institutional data associated with factors such as demographics, grades, and completion rates.

The initial findings of the evaluation data reveal that there was an increase in both the quantity and quality of interaction among the students and with the instructors (Vaughan & Garrison, 2006b). The design of group work was the primary reason for this increase. At the same time, students felt they required more guidance and structure, thus suggesting a need for clear expectations and support (that is, teaching presence). The postcourse interviews with faculty reinforced the previous findings as well as a need for an orientation to what constitutes a blended learning course. Finally, evaluation data provided strong support for the ITBL program, which offered insights to what others were doing, as well as project-specific support, tasks, and timelines for their course redesign.

It is not sufficient to simply change approaches without considering incentives and infrastructure as well. The essential first element of this transformation is to provide the incentives (financial, recognition, and reward) to reevaluate and redesign approaches to teaching and learning. Incentives are perhaps the most powerful change element. Redesign incentives were also complemented with reward-and-recognition incentives. Annual merit points were provided specifically for teaching performance and innovation. Equally important, recognition was given with teaching awards and consideration during promotion procedures. This support ensures both the long-term viability and success of the blended learning redesign initiative and the transformation of the institution's approach to teaching and learning.

Finally, physical spaces had to be redesigned to provide formal and informal collaborative learning opportunities. This began within the library facilities and the creation of an open learning commons. It progressed further with the expansion of the library and the addition of more collaborative work space that could be booked by students and staff for project work.

In summary, the following recommendations were offered to shape institutional change:

1. Raise institutional awareness, build support, and cultivate collaborative leadership
2. Develop institutional policy, strategic plans, and achievable goals
3. Provide sustained incentives and recognition
4. Build instructional development and course redesign support programs
5. Invest in technology infrastructure
6. Design prototypes and ensure early successes
7. Create systematic evaluation strategies and accountability procedures
8. Review learning spaces and scheduling practices
9. Establish continuous communication strategies
10. Keep senior administration informed and on board
11. Create a task group to address issues, challenges, and opportunities and recommend new directions
12. Update and refine policies, goals, and support programs

It is not an exaggeration that blended learning provides an opportunity to return to the fundamental values and practices of higher education. But this will only happen with sustained, decisive, collaborative leadership across the institution.

Conclusion

Communications and information technology has transformed, or is transforming, most of society. However, in higher education, for "the most part fundamental change has been shunned; universities have opted for cosmetic surgery...when radical reconstruction is called for" (Boyer Commission, 2001). Higher education institutions have yet to fully recognize the transformative impact and potential of communication and Internet technologies to concurrently address pedagogical and budget shortfalls. As Smith (2004) states: "The world that is emerging requires new instructional approaches, new organizational forms, and new academic cultures to meet its needs" (p. 30). The confluence of all three elements reflects the urgency for higher education to begin the change process.

Appendix 2

PROJECT PROPOSAL FORM

Course Development and Enhancement Project

Applicant Information—Lead Applicant

Name

Position

Department/faculty

E-mail

Phone

Office location

Mailing address

Collaborating Applicant Information—Encouraged

Name(s)

Position

Department/faculty

E-mail

Phone

Office location

Mailing address

Name(s)

Position

Department/faculty

E-mail

Phone

Office location

Mailing address

Submitted by

Lead applicant signature

Dean's signature

Please attach a brief statement of support from your dean or department head.

(Proposals will be evaluated by the Inquiry Learning Action Group.)

Please submit completed proposal to the Executive Suite, A100, c/o the VP (Academic).

Date received:

Part 1: Project Detail

Course Information

Name of course

Four-letter code and number if existing course

Is this a new course or a course for redesign?

Place the course in context in a short paragraph of 150 words or fewer. (*Describe student learning outcomes, content, primary teaching methods currently used—for example, undergraduate biology course, students gain basic knowledge and concepts primarily through readings, lectures, and inquiry projects.*)

How many sections of this course are typically offered each year?

How many students per section, on average?

What percentage of section instructors will be active in planning the redesign?

Time Frame

When will this new or revised inquiry or blended-learning course first be offered? Fall 2007 or Winter 2008 or Fall 2008 (please indicate one)

When will you begin to work on your design or redesign project?

Current Course Outline

Project Goals and Rationale (800 words or fewer). Articulate how this project involves innovative course design rather than simply a series of minor changes. Describe what you hope to accomplish with this project and list the primary goals. How will both effective pedagogy and resource efficiencies be realized? Describe your vision for this course as *inquiry*, how it may involve blended learning, how evaluation will be consonant with the inquiry aspect of the course, and how it contributes to the university's academic plan. Specifically, how it will assist your faculty and department? Please detail how you believe it will affect your teaching and your students' learning. Please indicate if the students taking the course will need any special resources (for example, daily computer access). Finally, what roles will TAs or other student assistants play in the redesigned course?

Why is this project important? What are the key design or redesign issues? How is blended learning essential to the improved delivery of this course? Who will be involved? What resources will be needed?

Redesign Process (250 words or fewer). How will this project involve all faculty, staff, or stakeholders important to ensuring success?

Part 2: Project Evaluation and Sustainability Plans (approximately 1 page).

Evaluation Plan (250 words or fewer)

List each of your project's goals and describe your plan for assessing the extent to which they are being achieved. The analysis of these data should allow you to make evidence-based claims about the efficacy of your intervention, and it would provide guideposts for future redesign. The Teaching and Learning Centre staff are available for consultation with regard to evaluation. Please note that in addition to these local evaluative measures, it is expected that all projects will be evaluated using the Inquiry and Blended Learning Student Survey, which the Teaching & Learning Centre has adapted from the National Survey of Student Engagement.

Sustainability Plan (250 words or fewer)

Assuming evaluation activities yield information to suggest that the course innovations should continue, what measures will you and your faculty or department take to ensure continuation and improvement? How will you share what you learn with others in your faculty?

Part 3: Budget Detail. If this award is intended to be applied toward release time for development, state who will be released, when, for how long, and at what projected cost. Detail any other funds that are being requested to complete the project. The anticipated maximum is $10,000 for ten projects and $30,000 for one large-enrollment course redesign.

Appendix 3

REDESIGN GUIDE FOR BLENDED LEARNING

1. **Analysis Phase (understanding the big picture and identifying what you want to preserve and transform in your course redesign)**

Questions	Comments	Status
a. What do you want your students to know when they have finished taking your blended learning course (e.g., key learning outcomes—knowledge, skills, and attitudes)?		
b. What do you want to preserve from your existing course format?		
c. What would you like to transform?		

2. **Design Phase (identifying learning activities, assessment plans, and key components for your course)**

Questions	Comments	Status
a. Blended teaching is not just a matter of transferring a portion of your current course to the Web. Instead it involves developing challenging and engaging learning activities that occur within and outside of the classroom. What types of learning activities will you design that integrate face-to-face (F2F) and time-out-of-class (TOC) components?		

(Continued)

Questions	Comments	Status
b. What means will you use to assess these integrated learning activities?		
c. What are your expectations for student participation within and outside of the classroom? How will you configure and schedule the percent of time between the F2F and TOC components of your course?		
d. How will you use your course outline to communicate the learning outcomes, activities, assessment plan, schedule, and key content topics to your students?		

3. Development Phase (creating the learning activities, assessment plan, and content for your course)

Questions	Comments	Status
a. How will you use a learning management system (i.e., Blackboard) to create a structure for your course (e.g., content modules, key topic areas)?		
b. What existing resources can you use for your blended course (e.g., existing handouts, digital learning objects)?		
c. What new learning activities and/or content do you need to develop for your course?		

4. Implementation Phase (actual course delivery—"where the rubber hits the road")

Questions	Comments	Status
a. Have you contacted the Registrar's Office about scheduling and approving the format of your blended course?		

(Continued)

Questions	Comments	Status

b. When students are involved in TOC activities within a blended course, they frequently have problems scheduling their work and managing their time. What plans do you have to help students address these issues?

c. Students sometimes have difficulty with Blackboard and other educational technologies. What proactive steps can you take to assist students to become familiar with these forms of technology? If students need help with technology in your course, how will you provide support?

5. Evaluation Phase (determining the effectiveness of the blended learning course and disseminating the results)

Questions	Comments	Status

a. What kind of assessments and data collection are you planning in order to effectively evaluate your project and inform efforts to improve the course in future offerings (e.g., midterm evaluations, peer-observation and feedback, journal, teaching assessments, evaluations of student learning, student ratings of instruction)?

b. Assuming evaluation activities yield information to suggest your blended learning course should continue, what measures will you and your faculty or department take to ensure the continuation and improvement of the course? How will you share what you learn with others in your faculty?

Appendix 4

BLENDED FACULTY COMMUNITY OF INQUIRY PLANNING DOCUMENT

1. Program Goal

The successful redesign and implementation of university credit courses in a blended delivery format. Within such a blended learning course a significant portion of the learning activities have been moved online, and time traditionally spent in the classroom is reduced but not eliminated. The goal of these blended courses is to join the best features of in-class teaching with the best features of online learning to promote active, self-directed learning and reduce class seat time.

2. Program Outcomes

Program Outcomes for a Blended Faculty Community of Inquiry

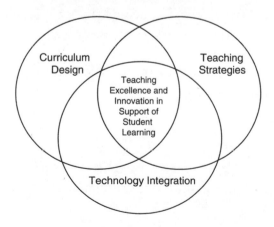

Curriculum Design. A curriculum redesign plan of a university credit course for blended learning. This plan involves the

Formulation of a blended course vision and learning outcomes

Development of a course syllabus

Development of online learning activities (in modular format), which integrate with the face-to-face sessions of the course

Creation of assignments based on the identified learning outcomes

Development of a course assessment plan based on the identified learning outcomes

Assembling of a grading criteria for the course based on the identified learning outcomes and the course assessment strategy

Development of a set of student interaction protocols (for email, discussions) to be followed in the course

Draft of specific tactics for developing a "learning community" in the course

Devising a strategy for implementing "learning support" in the course

Teaching Strategies. The acquisition of effective face to face and online teaching skills and strategies such as

Facilitating and directing online discussions

Stimulating online communication

Managing group work

Assessing online work

Directing students to appropriate support personnel and/or resource documentation for time management and study skills

Technology Integration. The acquisition of technology skills such as

1. Managing a course Web site by being able to successfully manipulate the following features:

    Course content—Adding and revising course content (announcements, course information, course documents, linking to external resources such as digital learning objects)

    User management—Enrolling, listing, and removing students into the course site and group areas

    Tools—Communication and collaboration features, digital drop box, course calendar

    Assessment features—Online testing and survey tools, online grade book and course statistics

    Site design and functionality—Adding and editing navigational buttons

2. Troubleshooting basic student technology issues:

    Login and password problems

    Directing students to proper support personnel and/or resource documentation for hardware (computer), software (applications and plug-ins), and connectivity (Internet service provider) issues

3. Tentative Blended Faculty Community of Inquiry Schedule

a) **Presession Work over the Summer**

- Answer the following questions over the summer and bring your responses to our kick-off session in August

    What do you want to preserve in your course?

    What do you want to change with your course?

- Take the Teaching Goals Inventory online for your focus course, print out the results, and bring it to our August kick-off session. The URL is http://www. uiowa.edu/~centeach/tgi/.

b) **Kick-off Session Agenda**

- Knowledge probe (before session)—Teaching Goals Inventory
- Introduction to the faculty learning community and each other
- Blended Learning

  What is it, and do you plan to operationalize this concept within your redesigned course?

  What are the advantages and challenges for the students and faculty involved with this project?

- Sharing initial thoughts and ideas about each other's projects
- Orientation to the Blended Faculty CoI Web site, which will be used for this program
- Take away questions for online discussion:

  What do you want students to know when they have finished taking your blended course?

  As you think about learning outcomes, which would be better achieved online, and which would be best achieved face-to-face?

- Session outcomes—clear understanding of blended learning, the objectives of this blended faculty CoI program, the time, commitment, and workload involved

c) **Fall Sessions (Six ninety-minute face-to-face sessions combined with a series of online activities and assignments)**

- Fall Semester: Project outcomes—completed course redesign plan, course syllabus (objectives, assignments, assessment plan, grading criteria), and a functional course Web site shell with one prototype module.

d) **Winter Sessions (Six ninety-minute face-to-face sessions combined with a series of online activities and assignments)**

Session	Topic	Discussion Component	Lab Component
One	Identifying key learning outcomes	What will students remember five years after the course?	Creation of a course menu structure within your course Web site
Two	Designing integrated face-to-face and online learning activities	Designing and developing learning activities Seven principles of effective teaching practice Using technology to leverage these principles	Management and manipulation of the learning management system tools such as the communication and collaboration features, digital drop box, course calendar
Three	Developing a course assessment strategy	Web-based assessment techniques and activities	Assessment tools in the learning management system—testing, surveys, online grade book, and course statistics
Four	Creating a learning-centered course syllabus (redesign plan)	Course syllabus—your redesign plan	Using Web editors to create html pages—Microsoft Word, Macromedia Dreamweaver
Five	Developing a course module prototype	Developing a paper-based course module prototype	Using Adobe Photoshop to create banners and buttons for your course modules
Six	Leveraging the use of digital learning object repositories	Digital learning objects — "Legos of Learning"	Creating external links within your course Web site to learning objects

Session	Topic	Discussion Component	Lab Component
Seven	Developing your own digital learning objects	Low threshold applications (LTAs)	Demonstration and construction of Audio and video clips Narrated PowerPoint presentations Basic animations
Eight	Facilitating and directing online learning	Creating student interaction protocols, activities, and assessment rubrics	Communication tools within the learning management system, asynchronous and synchronous
Nine	Integrating face-to-face and online activities	Activities to "glue" the face-to-face (F2F) and time-out-of-class (TOC) components	Construction of just in time teaching techniques (JITT) Classroom assessment techniques (CATs) within your course Web site
Ten	Learner support strategies	Developing a learning community	Student orientation to your blended learning course Student time and study management strategies and skills
Eleven	Piloting and course evaluation strategies	Piloting and course evaluation strategies	Experimentation with digital survey collection tools Survey tool within the learning management system Flashlight assessment program (FAST—free assessment summary tool)
Twelve	Show & tell (project demonstration) session for the university community		

Project outcomes—a redesigned course, a course Web site, and the necessary teaching and educational technology strategies and skills to create a successful blended learning environment for your students.

Appendix 5

STUDENT SURVEY QUESTIONNAIRE

Important Note: The purpose of this survey is to gather student responses that will help inform the ongoing development of this and other blended learning courses at the University of Calgary. Participation in this survey is voluntary and your responses will be kept confidential and anonymous. Nonparticipation in this study will not jeopardize student progress in this course. Completion of the questionnaire below will constitute informed consent in this inquiry and blended learning evaluation study.

The University of Calgary Conjoint Faculties Research Ethics Board has approved this research study. The survey results will be stored on a secure Teaching & Learning Centre server, access will be restricted to the researchers involved in this study, and the data will be destroyed when it is deemed irrelevant by the researchers. Data obtained from this study may be used by the researchers in academic publications and presentations.

1. Place in program: ☐ First Year ☐ Second Year ☐ Third Year ☐ Fourth Year ☐ Graduate

2. Student status: ☐ Full Time ☐ Part Time

3. Number of courses taken this semester: ＿＿＿＿＿＿＿

4. Place of residence: ☐ On-campus residency ☐ Commuting from off-campus

5. Work status: ☐ Full Time ☐ Part Time ☐ None

6. Age: ＿＿＿＿＿＿＿

7. Gender: ☐ Female ☐ Male

8. What was your primary reason for choosing this blended learning course?

☐ Convenience of not having to come to campus as often

☐ Flexibility of being able to complete assignments anyplace/anytime

☐ It is a required course

☐ It was the only available option course that fit into my timetable

☐ I chose the instructor, not the course modality

☐ Job responsibilities make it difficult for me to attend face-to-face classes

☐ I have a disability that makes travel inconvenient

☐ Other (please specify):

9. In comparison to the interaction experienced with students and instructors in other courses, how would you describe the **amount** of interaction experienced with:

	Increased	Somewhat Increased	No Difference	Somewhat Decreased	Decreased
Other students in this blended learning course					
Comments:					
The *instructor* in this blended learning course					
Comments:					

10. In comparison to the interaction experienced with students and instructors in other courses, how would you describe the **quality** of interaction experienced with:

Other students in this blended learning course				
Comments:				
The *instructor* in this blended learning course				
Comments:				

Indicate how strongly you agree or disagree with the following statements:

Statement	Strongly Agree	Agree	Not Sure	Disagree	Strongly Disagree
11. Blended learning courses are sufficiently identified and expectations made clear in the U of C course calendar.					
Comments:					

Statement	Strongly Agree	Agree	Not Sure	Disagree	Strongly Disagree
12. The U of C provides sufficient resources for this specific blended course.					
Comments:					
13. Given the opportunity I would take another blended learning course in the future.					
Comments:					
14. Overall, I am satisfied with this blended learning course.					
Comments:					

Statement	Too Light	Light	Moderate	Heavy	Too Heavy
15. Compared to your other courses was the workload in this course:					
Comments:					

Statement	Online and in-class work enhanced each other.	Online and in-class work were relevant to each other.	The connection between the two was not always clear.	There was little or no connection between the two.
16. How would you describe the relationship between the online and in class learning in this course?				
Comments:				

Please comment on the following questions:

17. How does this blended learning course differ from traditional classroom instruction?

18. What was the **most** effective aspect of this blended learning course?

19. What was the **least** effective aspect of this blended learning course?

20. What advice would you give to a student considering a blended learning course for the first time?

What suggestions can you provide to help strengthen this blended learning course?

Appendix 6

FACULTY INTERVIEW QUESTIONS

1. What were the key goals or outcomes of your inquiry and blended learning project?
2. What new learning activities or assessments did you use to attempt to achieve these goals or outcomes?
3. How did you use information and communication technologies to support this process?
4. What did blended learning mean or look like in your course?
5. How did you inform or orientate your students to inquiry and blended learning in your course?
6. What were the benefits to you of this redesigned course?
7. What were the challenges that you encountered with this redesigned course?
8. What will you do differently the next time you offer this course?
9. Lessons learned?
10. What advice would you like to pass onto to other faculty members who are planning to design and implement inquiry and blended learning courses?

Comments about support from the Teaching & Learning Centre:

Appendix 7

STUDENT SURVEY RESULTS

The following is a summary of results from the student survey questionnaire (Appendix 5) administered in eight blended learning courses at the end of the winter 2006 semester:

1. Response rate: 76% (241 of 316 potential students)

2. University status:

First Year	50%
Second Year	14%
Third Year	19%
Fourth Year	14%
Graduate	2%
Unclassified	0.8%
No response	0.4%

3. Gender:

Female	78.4%
Male	21.2%
No response	0.4%

4. Primary reason for choosing the blended learning course:

It is a required course	71.0%
Other (i.e., course topic sounded interesting)	13.3%
I chose the instructor, not the course modality	5.4%
It was the only available option course that fit into my timetable	3.7%
Flexibility of being able to complete assignments anyplace/anytime	2.9%
Convenience of not having to come to campus as often	2.5%
Job responsibilities make it difficult for me to attend face-to-face classes	0.8%
No response	0.4%
I have a disability that makes travel inconvenient	0.0%

5. Student perceptions

Statement	Agreed	No Difference	Disagreed	No Response
The quantity of interaction with other students was increased in this ITBL course compared to other courses.	78%	16%	5%	1%
The quality of interaction with other students was increased in this ITBL course compared to other courses.	69%	25%	4%	2%
The quality of interaction with the instructor was increased in this ITBL course compared to other courses	59%	28%	12%	1%
The quantity of interaction with the instructor was increased in this ITBL course compared to other courses	55%	28%	15%	2%
The U of C provided sufficient resources for this ITBL course	53%	27%	19%	1%
You were satisfied with this ITBL course	48%	23%	25%	4%
Given the opportunity you would take another ITBL course in the future	45%	27%	26%	2%
ITBL courses are sufficiently identified and expectations made clear in the U of C course calendar.	19%	36%	43%	2%

6. Most and least effective aspects of the ITBL courses

Most effective	Least effective
Group work (49)*	Lack of clear expectations, structure, organization and direction (67)
Discussions—face to face and online (30)	Online component (18)
Greater degree of interaction with other students and instructors (25)	Online discussions (15)
	Self-directed learning approach (13)
Online resources (25)	Increased workload (13)
Greater flexibility (13)	Poor or lack of communication (6)
New ways of learning (11)	Lectures (6)
Self-directed learning opportunities	Group work (5)
Instructors (9)	Overload of information and resources (5)
Applying what we learned (9)	Technological "glitches" and problems (5)
Course structure (5)	Lack of learning (4)
Variety of assignments and methods of assessment (5)	No ineffective elements (3)
Not effective (4)	Less physical presence (3)
Integration of online and in-class learning (3)	Lack of interaction (2)
	Lack of blended learning (2)
Guest speakers (3)	Guest speakers (1)
Unsure (2)	Boring course content (1)
Course readings (1)	
No difference (1)	

*( )—Indicate the number of related comments.

Appendix 8

FACULTY INTERVIEW COMMENTS

The following is a summary of results from the faculty interviews (Appendix 6) conducted with the instructors responsible for eight blended learning courses implemented during the winter 2006 semester:

1. Instructor benefits of the redesigned course:

    Experimented with new teaching strategies and tools

    Increased student interaction in the course

2. Instructor challenges encountered with this redesigned course:

    Increased workload for myself

    Student "push back" and resistance to taking increased responsibility for their learning

    Technology issues and challenges (e.g., Blackboard server problems)

3. Changes that will be made to the redesigned course for future implementations:

    Provide a more explicit and involved student orientation to inquiry and blended learning

    Ensure that my learning or assessment activities are aligned with my course objectives

    Focus more on the discipline inquiry process rather than on covering content in my course

Make sure that I develop a "clear plan" for the course and
that all my student learning resources and activities are
constructed before the class begins (not enough time to
properly develop these "on the fly" during a course)

4. Lessons learned:

Theme	Related Comment
A) Project Development Stage	
Importance of course redesign—complementary and integrated face-to-face and online activities	*Work online has to be linked to work done in class, in that it either sets up the in-class component or allows students to further consider the in-class elements.*
Build on your strengths	*Don't throw away things that have worked in the past. Use those as strengths to be built upon.*
Don't go it alone	*There's lots of help and support from the Teaching & Learning Centre and other faculty involved with ITBL projects.*
Use the resource material posted to our ITBL Blackboard site	*Read the information posted on the ITBL site. There is a lot of helpful stuff there!*
Openness to new ideas and a willingness to ask for feedback	*Be open to considering new ideas. Realize also that what might work for someone else might not work for you.*
Set project development goals and deadlines for yourself	*Consciously set a goal for each project meeting so that you get work done between them.*
Budget time to work on your project between the face-to-face sessions	*Set aside time on a regular basis to deal with information in between meetings*
Use existing resources—don't try and reinvent the wheel	*Utilize resources that are already constructed—Library of Congress material, MERLOT, CAREO, etc.*
Avoid the course and a half syndrome	*Blended learning is not an effective way to add more content to your course. It is a great way to alter the delivery of a course by offering students more options and independence.*

Theme	Related Comment
B) Project Delivery Tips	
Importance of informing students about your blended style of course delivery	*Ensure in the outline that students are aware that it will be blended delivery*
Importance of scheduling a student orientation to inquiry and blended learning	*These concepts are new to the majority of U of C students—be sure to inform students about the nature of your course—before they enroll and be sure to involve the students in a discussion about these concepts during the first week of your course*
Student engagement	*Blended learning doesn't necessarily mean glitzy Web pages or high-tech animations. It's about engaging students in their learning. Many Web-based tools are surprisingly simple, yet can be effective learning tools for students.*
Use of the Blackboard learning management system:	*More exposure to the options and uses of Blackboard allows for greater creativity in maximizing student learning opportunities*

5. Advice to other faculty members who are planning to design and implement ITBL courses:

> Be open to new ideas for teaching and learning

> Start "early" when preparing for your blended learning course

> Ask for help when you need it—take a "collaborative" rather than "solo" approach to redesigning your course for blended learning

6. Comments about support from the ITBL program:

> Lunch meetings provide "breadth" and opportunities to learn about a diversity of approaches to inquiry and blended learning

- Online components offer opportunities to reflect on how new ideas can be incorporated into the redesigned course
- Workshops present "hands-on" opportunities to develop learning resources for your blended learning course
- Individual project meetings provide "depth"; opportunity to discuss project-specific issues, set project milestones, and assign project related tasks

Appendix 9

TEMPLATE FOR PREPARING A BLENDED LEARNING COURSE OUTLINE

1. Course Information
   - Course title
   - Course number
   - Credits
   - Prerequisites or corequisites
   - Semester and year
   - Day and time
   - Location of the class
2. Faculty Information
   - Name
   - Contact information
     - Phone
     - E-mail (including response time—weekdays versus weekends)
     - Office hours
   - Course-related Web site
3. Course Description (from the calendar)
4. Textbook(s), Readings, and Course Materials
5. Learning Outcomes
   - Course learning outcomes with program outcomes embedded or separate

6. Methods of Blended Learning Instruction

   Indicate what blended learning means within this course

   Explain why this course is being offered in a blended learning format

   Describe some of the challenges that students might face in this blended learning course

   Provide a listing of institutional support that is available to help students succeed within this type of learning environment

7. Methods of Assessment

   Methods used in this course to assess students

   Assessment approaches are linked to stated learning outcomes

   Assignments are weighted (if applicable)

   Criteria for how students will be graded on each assessment (may be attached as appendices or in a special assignment handout)

   The grading scheme used

8. Course Policies

   Attendance, punctuality, and participation

   Missed exams and assignments

   Integrity of student work (i.e., plagiarism)

   Reference to key statements in the institutional calendar

9. Tentative Course Schedule and Related Readings

   Key dates

Appendix 10

SAMPLE BLENDED LEARNING COURSE OUTLINE

Introduction to Computers in Education (EDUC 3325.001)

1. Course Information

Course Title:	Introduction to Computers in Education
Course Number:	EDUC3325.001
Credits:	4
Prerequisites:	EDUC2231 and EDUC2233
Transferability:	University of Calgary, University of Lethbridge, University of Alberta

2. Faculty Information

Faculty:	**Phone:**	**E-mail:**	**Office:**
Dr. Norm Vaughan	220–7811	nvaughan@ ucalgary.ca	EA3014
Lecture Time:	Monday 17:00 to 19:50 pm	Lab: E141	
Tutorial Time:	Wednesday 17:00 to 18:50 pm	Lab: E141	
Office Hours:	By appointment (please phone or e-mail in advance)		
Blackboard Course Web Site:	Can be accessed through MyMRC (http://www. mymrc.ca) or directly through the Blackboard Server (http:// courseware.mymrc.ca)		

3. Course Description

An introduction to the theoretical and practical components of computers in education with particular reference to their academic, social, and cultural implications. The practical component exposes students to different computing environments and several software packages.

4. Course Materials

The readings and handouts can be accessed through the EDUC3325 Blackboard site. Print copies of all the handouts will be provided in the lectures. Your Mount Royal College fee covers the cost of open lab supervision. However, use of the laser printer inside and outside of class time involves using your SmartCard (http://www.mtroyal.ab.ca/smartcard/index.shtml).

Remember, magnetic media is not always reliable—always back-up your work.

5. Learning Outcomes

Through the application of course content, your participation in the learning activities, and the related assessment techniques, you should be able to:

1. **Emphasize *computer literacy skills* that will support your ability to integrate technology into your future teaching practice by having:**

   - Basic knowledge about computer technology (general grasp of how computers work and ability to use basic computer terminology)
   - Equipment operations skills (e.g., formatting disks, loading and running programs, saving files, printing documents, and trouble shooting for minor problems)
   - Productivity tools skills (ability to use and teach word processing, database, spreadsheet software)
   - Instructional application skills (evaluate and use various types of specialized computer software—drill and practice, tutorial, simulation, and problem-solving)

- Management application skills (use computers to manage and complete tasks such as record keeping, progress reports, report cards, attendance, worksheets, tests, letters to parents, and grade books)

2. **Emphasize *communication skills* that will encourage your ability to communicate ideas and opinions by:**

- Communicating clearly and concisely using written, spoken, visual, or computer-based formats and media appropriate to the situation and audience needs
- Demonstrating interpersonal skills by listening effectively, establishing rapport, and monitoring non-verbal signals
- Interpreting and evaluating meaning using a variety of computer based texts and media formats

3. **Emphasize *group effectiveness skills* that will support the notion of a collaborative learning culture using technology by:**

- Participating in specific group tasks and by using technology to build relationships to support group effectiveness
- Communicating effectively in a group setting by listening actively and giving and receiving feedback appropriately
- Demonstrating personal group effectiveness by being open, flexible, respectful of others, and accepting of diversity

4. Method of Instruction—Blended Learning

What Does Blended Learning Mean in This Course?

This course will be offered in a blended format incorporating teaching and learning activities which use information communications technologies such as the Internet, significantly reducing the scheduled face-to-face lecture and tutorial time.

You will be working with a Web-based learning management system called Blackboard which will be introduced during the first stages of the course. Materials and assignments will be provided through this EDUC3325 course site. Discussion groups will be formed and as a member you will participate in online conference sessions with others. You will also be expected to use e-mail to respond to the course instructor and peers about assigned topics.

This course has a tutorial component. Tutorial activities will primarily be conducted within the Blackboard course site, outside of face-to-face class time. As a part of the tutorial, you will be given assignments to complete using a variety of software applications. Some assignments will be group intensive while others will be individual. Completed assignments will be part of your final mark.

Why Is This Course Being Offered in the Blended Learning Format?

The goals of this course are to:

1. Promote active, self-directed learning by providing you with an effective combination of in-class teaching and online learning.

2. Shift some topics into the online format with a resultant reduction in face-to-face time.

3. Use the reduced lecture and tutorial hours more efficiently to focus on the material that is more effectively presented in a face-to-face format.

4. Provide you with more flexibility by allowing you to do more of your work from home and to complete online learning activities at times that best suit your weekly schedule and learning preferences.

What Are Some of the Challenges That Students Might Face in a Blended Learning Course?

It is important to remember that:

1. All students in this course must have daily access to the Internet. You must use the Blackboard site regularly between classes to keep up with the announcements and to complete the assigned activities.

2. Less time spent in lectures and tutorials does NOT mean less work. You may find that the time spent in online activities will be considerable, but it is expected that your active participation will enhance your learning.

3. Learning is not a spectator sport. You are expected to take the responsibility to actively use the online learning material and to manage your time so that you complete assigned reading and online activities between the face-to-face sessions.

   Please read this entire course outline thoroughly and return the contract on the last page to your instructor by the end of the second week of classes.

What Kind of Support Is Available for This Blended Learning Course?

1. Study and Time Management Skills

   Face-to-face support is available through the Learning Skills Centre (T123) from Monday to Friday (08:30 to 16:30) or online at: http://www.mtroyal.ca/learningskills/

2. Library Services

   The Instructional Librarian assigned to this EDUC3325 course is Pearl Herscovitch. She can be contacted by phone (440- 6022) or email (pherscovitch@mtroyal.ca). Online resources related to this course are also available at: http://library.mtroyal.ca/instruction/05–06/educ3325.htm

3. Information Technology Services (ITS)

   ### Online Learning Orientation

   A series of Web-based tutorials (http://www.acad.mtroyal.ca/onlineorientation/) designed to provide you with an introduction and review of the basic computing skills needed to learn in a blended learning environment at MRC utilizing such tools

as Blackboard, MyMRC, On-line Library services, and a review
of some basic computing skills. Resources are also provided to
ensure that the off-campus computer that you are using will be
compatible with the MRC computer learning environment.

Computer Labs

Open Student Computer Labs are available for your use
outside of regular class/tutorial time (http://www.mtroyal.ca/
studentlife/labs.shtml)

	EA2047	E151	EB1112	Library	T248
Monday–Thursday	8:30 a.m.–7:00 p.m.	8:00 a.m.–10:00 p.m.	8:30 a.m.–7:00 p.m.	7:45 a.m.–10:00 p.m.	9:00 a.m.–5:00 p.m.
Friday	8:30 a.m.–5:00 p.m.	8:00 a.m.–5:00 p.m.	8:30 a.m.–5:00 p.m.	7:45 a.m.–5:00 p.m.	9:00 a.m.–5:00 p.m.
Saturday	Closed	11:00 a.m.–5:00 p.m.	Closed	9:00 a.m.–5:00 p.m.	Closed
Sunday	Closed	11:00 a.m.–5:00 p.m.	Closed	1:00 p.m.–5:00 p.m.	Closed

After-Hours Access

In order to access a lab that is monitored by a card reader (except
the drop-in labs) you need to get your SmartCard activated at the
security office located at the West Gate entrance. You must take
a copy of your class schedule, which shows that you are registered
in a course that requires lab access.

Student Computing Support

On-campus student computer training support is available
through the START (student technology and resource tu-
tor program: http://www.mtroyal.ca/programs/academserv/ADC/
start.html)

Contact Information
Room T106
Phone 440–7214
Email rscaddan@mtroyal.ca

Hours of Operation
Monday to Thursday from 10 a.m. to 6 p.m.
Friday from 10 a.m. to 3:00 p.m.

Questions about student computer issues such as logon and password problems can be answered through the **College's Help Desk**:

Contact Information	**Hours of Operation**
Room E251	Monday to Thursday from 8:00 a.m. to 7:00 p.m.
Phone 440–6034	Friday from 8:00 a.m. to 5:00 p.m.
Email helpdesk	Saturday 8:30 a.m. to 12:30 p.m.
@mtroyal.ca	

Remember that technology is wonderful but not intelligent; it may quit on you unexpectedly! Patience and tolerance are virtues you should cultivate in this technological society.

7. Methods of Assessment

A summative grade for the course will be determined by the following components:

Category	Percentage	Due Date
a) Tutorial Assignments		
Reading Activities	5	Throughout the course
Internet Lesson Plan	10	Jan 25
Spreadsheet	5	Jan 25
PowerPoint	5	Feb 1
Web-Based Student Portfolio	10	Feb 27
WebQuest	10	March 22
b) Online Discussions		
Participation	5	Throughout the course
Moderation and Summary	5	Assigned week
Reflection	5	Throughout the course
c) Teaching Presentation	15	April 10
d) Final Examination	25	April 19
Total	100	

College regulations require all scores be provided with a letter grade equivalent. This will be determined from the numerical marks assigned during the course as follows:

Grade	Grade Point Values	Percentage
A+	4.0	95–100
A	4.0	90–94
A–	3.7	85–89
B+	3.3	80–84
B	3.0	75–79
B–	2.7	70–74
C+	2.4	65–69
C	2.0	62–64
C-	1.7	59–61
D+	1.3	55–58
D	1.0	50–54
F	0.0	49 or less

8. Key Course Policies

Attendance/Punctuality and Participation

Missing scheduled face-to-face classes will most likely hamper your learning process, increasing the likelihood of lower grades. Because new concepts are taught each week and accompanying assignments build on these, it is extremely important that you master the skills set out weekly so you do not fall behind. Your course instructor has determined that students who miss face-to-face classes or leave tutorial periods early generally do not perform well. Students are responsible for participating in the assigned online learning activities throughout the semester.

Missed Assignments and Exams

There will be no opportunities to make up missed assignments or tests beyond the deadlines without a medical certificate. Assignments handed in late will be docked 1 full mark per day and will not be accepted after the following Monday of the week that they were due. Air flights or vacations, which conflict with exams or assignment deadlines, are not valid reasons for deferral.

Integrity of Student Work

The Mount Royal College Code of Student Conduct details the College's expectations of its students with respect to academic integrity and non-academic misconduct. The code of contact can be accessed online: http://www.mtroyal.ab.ca/codeofstudentconduct/

Academic Policies and Procedures

All students are responsible for familiarizing themselves with the College's academic policies, procedures, and regulations. These are published in the College Calendar and Schedule of Classes. They are also available online: http://www.mtroyal.ab.ca/studentlife/academic_policies.shtml

Instructor E-mail Responses

The instructor will reply to all student emails within a 24 hour period from Monday to Friday.

9. Tentative Course Schedule

Dates	Monday (Lecture)	Readings	Wednesday (Tutorial)
Jan. 2–4	Holiday—No Lecture	Handouts	Overview of the course and an orientation to the PC computer and the course Blackboard site
Jan. 9–11	Introduction to Internet Lesson Planning (classroom based)	Handouts	Introduction to Searching & the Internet (classroom based tutorial by Pearl Herscovitch from the Library)
Jan. 16–18	Using Technology Productivity Tools (classroom based)	Web-based articles	Microsoft Excel Spreadsheets & Internet Lesson Plan (online work)

Dates	Monday (Lecture)	Readings	Wednesday (Tutorial)
Jan. 23–25	Using Instructional Software (classroom based)	Web-based articles	MS PowerPoint (online work) *Hand in Internet Lesson Plan & Spreadsheet Assignment via the Digital Drop Box*
Jan. 30–Feb.1	Transforming the Learning Experience (classroom based)	Web-based articles	Web-based student portfolio (classroom based) *Hand in PowerPoint Assignment via the Digital Drop Box*
Feb. 6–8	Web-based student portfolio (online work)	Handouts	Web-based student portfolio (online work)
Feb. 13–15	Using Technology to Link Learners—Part One (types of telecommunications systems—classroom based)	Handouts	Web-based student portfolio (online work)
Feb. 20–22	Reading Week (on lecture or tutorial)		
Feb. 27–March 1	Using Technology to Link Learners—Part Two (online teaching activities—classroom based) *Hand in Web Portfolio Assignment via Digital Drop Box*	Handouts	WebQuests (online work)
March 6–8	Using Technology to Link Learners—Part Three (using CMC—online work)	Handouts	WebQuests (online work)
March 13–15	Integrating Technologies Across the Curriculum (classroom based)	Web-based articles	WebQuests (online work)

Dates	Monday (Lecture)	Readings	Wednesday (Tutorial)
March 20–22	Future Directions of Educational Technology (classroom based)	Handouts	Preparation for Group Teaching Presentations (online work) *Hand in Web Quest Assignment*
March 27–29	Preparation for Group Teaching Presentations (online work)		Preparation for Group Teaching Presentations (online work)
April 3–5	Preparation for Group Teaching Presentations (classroom based)		Preparation for Group Teaching Presentations (online work) *Submit your Weblog Reflections—Online Discussion Forum and Course Assignments*
April 10–12	*Group Teaching Presentations* (classroom based)		Final Exam Review (classroom based)
April 19	Final Exam will be on Wednesday April 19 from 19:00 to 21:00 in lab E141		

10. Key Dates at Mount Royal College

The Academic Schedule which includes the registration/withdrawal, fee payment, and holiday dates is available online: http://www.mtroyal.ab.ca/admission/academic_schedule.shtml

Welcome to the blended-delivery section of EDUC3325

Please read the course outline thoroughly, and complete and sign the following **Acknowledgment**. Return this to your instructor before the end of the first full week of classes.

By signing this Acknowledgment, I [print name] _____ **agree to the following:**

1. I have received and read the course outline for the blended delivery section of EDUC3325.

2. I have daily access to the Internet, either on a home computer or college computer.

3. I understand that this course contains components that are suited to students who are interested in active, self-directed learning.

4. I agree that the time-flexibility that will allow me to complete online activities at times that best suit my weekly schedule and learning preferences will also demand that I plan and manage my time efficiently. I take responsibility to actively use the online learning material and to manage my time so that I complete assigned reading and online activities before the deadlines.

5. I understand that, depending on my experience and skill level, the time required in utilizing the online material may vary among students. I am willing to expend extra time to initially familiarize myself with the online course environment.

6. I understand that it is my responsibility to use the course Blackboard site regularly between classes throughout the semester in order to stay informed regarding course announcements, individual and group assignments, and due dates.

Signature: _____ Date: _____

Appendix 11

SAMPLE ASSSESSMENT RUBRIC FOR AN E-PORTFOLIO ASSIGNMENT

Component	Beginning	Developing	Accomplished	Score

Home Page	0.5 points
	
	Incomplete—missing components and broken hyperlinks
		1.5 points
		
		All components are present and functional:
		• Your name
		• A graphical image (e.g., a picture of you or an image that represents something about you)
		• A paragraph, bulleted or numbered list of information about your teaching interests and aspirations
		• Horizontal lines to divide up the various sections of your page
		• Hypertext links to your:
		  ○ Resource page
		  ○ Lesson Plan
		  ○ PowerPoint Presentation
		  ○ Weblog (online journal)
			2 points
			
			Appropriate and thematic graphic elements are used to make visual connections that contribute to the understanding of concepts, ideas and relationships. Differences in type size and/or color are used well and consistently.
			
			The page content demonstrates reflection and connections with course content.	

Component	Beginning	Developing	Accomplished	Score
Resource Page	0.5 points Incomplete—missing components and broken hyperlinks	1.5 points All components are present and functional: • A title • At least one graphical image • At least five hypertext links to external educational WWW sites that support your teaching interests. Each of these links should include a title and a brief annotation (explanation/summary) about the Web site • A return link to your title (home) page	2 points There is a clear theme (e.g., subject area, grade level) to your resource links and the annotations provide a clear overview to each of the external Web sites.	
Lesson Plan Page	0.5 points Incomplete—missing components and broken hyperlinks	1.5 point All components are present and functional: • A title • At least one graphical image • A link to your actual lesson plan (and return link to your lesson plan menu page) • Personal reflections about your lesson plan • A brief summary of the lesson • Comments about what you learned from this assignment • Ideas and insights about how you will apply what you learned from this assignment (e.g., What will I do differently for my next lesson plan?) • A return link to your title (home) page	2 points The page content demonstrates meaningful and substantive reflection and connections with course content.	

Component	Beginning	Developing	Accomplished	Score

Powerpoint Page	0.5 points
	
	Incomplete—missing components and broken hyperlinks
		• 1.5 points
		• All components are present and functional:
		  ○ A title
		  ○ At least one graphi-cal image
		  ○ A link to your converted PowerPoint presentation assignment.
		• Personal reflections about your PowerPoint presentation, which should include:
		  ○ A brief summary of the presentation
		  ○ A return link to your title (home) page
			2 points
			The page content demonstrates meaningful and substantive reflection and connections with course content.	

Web-log (on-line journal)	0.5 points
	
	Incomplete—missing reflection entries and broken hyperlinks
		• 1.5 points
		• All components are present and functional:
		
		• Personal reflections:
		  ○ What did you learn in the process of creating your Web-based portfolio?
		  ○ What future plans do you have for your portfolio (or what would you do differently if you had to create a portfolio again)?
			2 points
			Substantive reflections and connections with course content.
			
			In addition, the Weblog should also include a minimum of 4 entries (Web-Portfolio, Power-Point, Spreadsheet and Lesson Plan Assignment reflections).	

Component	Beginning	Developing	Accomplished	Score
Web-log (on-line journal)		• Peer shared reflections (each of you will randomly select one other person in our course to provide feedback on his or her portfolio): ◦ What did you learn from reviewing this portfolio? ◦ What did you like about this portfolio? ◦ What recommendations or advice would you like to share with the person who created this portfolio (e.g., future plans, ways to make the portfolio even better)? • Weblog opens in a new browser window		
Total Score				/10

REFERENCES

Abrams, Z. (2005). ACMC, collaboration and the development of critical thinking in a graduate seminar in applied linguistics. *Canadian Journal of Learning Technology*, 31(2), 23–47.

Albrecht, B. (2006). Enriching student experience through blended learning. *Research Bulletin*, 12, EDUCAUSE Centre for Applied Research. http://www.educause.edu/ir/library/pdf/ecar_so/erb/ERB0612.pdf

Andrade, H. G. (2000). Using rubrics to promote thinking and learning. *Educational Leadership*, 57(5), 13–18.

Arabasz, P., & Baker, M. B. (2003). Evolving campus support models for e-learning courses. *Educause Center for Applied Research Bulletin*. Online: http://www.educause.edu/ir/library/pdf/ecar_so/ers/ERS0303/EKF0303.pdf

Arbaugh, J. B. (2006). *An empirical verification of the community of inquiry framework*. Paper presented to the Sloan Consortium Asynchronous Learning Network Invitational Workshop, Baltimore, MD, August.

Arbaugh, J. B. (2007). *Does the community of inquiry framework predict outcomes in online MBA courses?* Paper presented at the 2007 meetings of the Academy of Management, Management Education and Development Division, Philadelphia, PA, August.

Assessment Reform Group (2002). *Assessment for Learning: 10 Principles—research-based principles to guide classroom practice*. United Kingdom: The Qualifications and Curriculum Authority.

Ausubel, D. P. (1968). *Educational psychology: A cognitive view*. New York: Holt, Rinehart and Winston.

Banta, T. W. (2003). Introduction: Why Portfolios? In T. W. Banta (Ed.), *Portfolio assessment: Uses, cases, scoring and impact*. San Francisco: Jossey-Bass.

Barkley, E. F., Cross, K. P., and Major, C. H. (2005). *Collaborative learning techniques: A handbook for college faculty*. San Francisco: Jossey-Bass.

Barrett, H.C. (2004). *Differentiating electronic portfolios and online assessment management systems*. Paper presented at the annual meeting of the American Educational Research Association: San Diego, CA.

Bean, J. C. (1996). *Engaging ideas: The professor's guide to integrating writing, critical thinking, and active learning in the classroom.* San Francisco: Jossey-Bass.

Benbunan-Fich, R., & Arbaugh, J. B. (2006). Separating the effects of knowledge construction and group collaboration in web-based courses. *Information & Management, 43,* 778–793.

Beuchot, A., & Bullen, M. (2005). Interaction and interpersonality in online discussion forums. *Distance Education, 26*(1), 67–87.

Bonk, C. J., & Graham, C. R. (2006). *The handbook of blended learning: Global perspectives, local designs.* San Francisco: Pfeiffer.

Bonk, C. J., Kim, K., & Zeng, T. (2006). Future directions of blended learning in higher education and workplace learning settings. In C. J. Bonk, & C. R. Graham (Eds.), *The handbook of blended learning: Global perspectives, local design* (pp. 550–567). San Francisco: Pfeiffer.

Bourne, K., & Seaman, J. (2005). *Sloan-C special survey report: A look at blended learning.* Needham, MA: The Sloan Consortium.

Boyer Commission on Educating Undergraduates in the Research University (2001). *Reinventing undergraduate education: A blueprint for America's research university.* Retrieved September 6, 2001, from http://naples.cc.sunysb.edu/Pres/boyer.nsf/

Boyle, J. E. (1994). Portfolios: Purposes and possibilities. *Assessment Update, 6*(Sept.–Oct. 1994), 10–11.

Brookfield, S. D., and Preskill, S. (2005). *Discussion as a way of teaching: Tools and techniques for democratic classrooms* (2nd ed.). San Francisco: Jossey-Bass.

Brown, J. S., & Duguid, P. (2000). *The social life of information.* Boston, MA: Harvard Business School Press.

Brown, R. E. (2001). The process of community-building in distance learning classes. *Journal of Asynchronous Learning Networks, 5*(2), 18–35.

Burbules, N. C. (2004). Way of thinking about educational quality. *Educational Researcher, 33*(6), 4–10.

Cagle, A. B., & Hornik, S. (2001). Faculty development and educational technology. *T.H.E. Journal, 29*(3), 92–96.

Camblin, L. D. Jr., & Steger, J. A. (2000). Rethinking faculty development. *Higher Education, 39,* 1–18.

Celentin, P. (2007). Online training: Analysis of interaction and knowledge building patterns among foreign language teachers. *Journal of Distance Education, 21*(3), 39–58.

Chickering, A. W., & Gamson, Z. F. (1987). Seven principles for good practice in undergraduate education. *AAHE Bulletin, 39*(7), 3–7.

Collins, J. (2001). *Good to great: Why some companies make the leap and others don't.* New York: HarperCollins.

Conrad, D. (2005). Building and maintaining community in cohort-based online learning. *Journal of Distance Education*, 20(1), 1–20.

Coppola, N. W., Hiltz, S. R., & Rotter, N. (2002). Becoming a virtual professor. Pedagogical roles and asynchronous learning networks. *Journal of Management Information Systems*, 18(4), 169–190.

Cox, M. D. (2002). Achieving teaching and learning excellence through faculty learning communities. *Essays on Teaching Excellence: Toward the Best in the Academy*, 14(4). http://www.podnetwork.org/publications&resources/academy.htm

Cox, M. D. (2004). Introduction to faculty learning communities. In M. D. Cox & L. Richlin (Eds.), *Building faculty learning communities*. New Directions for Teaching and Learning, no. **97**, 5–23. San Francisco: Jossey-Bass.

Crouch, C. H., & Mazur, E. (2001). Peer instruction: Ten years of experience and results. *American Journal of Physics*, 69, 970–977.

Dewey, J. (1933). *How we think* (rev. ed.). Boston: D.C. Heath.

Dewey, J. (1959). My pedagogic creed. In *J. Dewey: Dewey on education* (pp. 19–32). New York: Teachers College, Columbia University. (Original work published 1897)

Dewey, J. (1981). *The Philosophy of John Dewey. Volume 2: The lived experience.* John J. McDermott (Ed.), University of Chicago Press, Chicago.

Dewey, J., & Childs, J. L. (1981). The underlying philosophy of education. In J. A. Boydston (Ed.), *John Dewey: The later works, 1925–1953, Vol. 8* (pp. 77–103). Carbondale: Southern Illinois University Press. (Original work published 1933).

Dixon, J. S., Crooks, H., & Henry, K. (2006). Breaking the ice: Supporting collaboration and the development of community online. *Canadian Journal of Learning and Technology*, 32(2), 99–117.

Dixson, M., Kuhlhorst, M., & Reiff, A. (2006). Creating effective online discussions: Optimal instructor and student roles. *Journal of Asynchronous Learning Networks*, 10(3), 15–28.

Drucker, P. F. (1999). *Management challenges for the 21st century.* New York: HarperCollins.

Duderstadt, J. J., Atkins, D. E., & Van Houweling, D. (2002). *Higher education in the digital age: Technology issues and strategies for American colleges and universities.* Westport, CT: Greenwood Press.

Dziuban, C., Hartman, J., Moskal, P., Sorg, S., & Truman, B. (2004). Three ALN modalities: An institutional perspective. In J. Bourne & J. C. Moore (Eds.), *Elements of Quality Online Education: Into the Mainstream* (pp. 127–148). Needham, MA: Sloan Center for OnLine Education.

Dziuban, C., Moskal, P., & Hartman, J. (2006). *Higher education, blended learning and the generations: Knowledge is power no more.* Proceedings of the Sloan-C Workshop on Blended Learning and Higher Education, Chicago, May.

Entwistle, N., McCune, V., & Hounsell, J. (2003). Investigating ways of enhancing university teaching-learning environments: Measuring students' approaches to studying and perceptions of teaching. In E. De Corte, L. Verschaffel, N. Entwistle, & J. van Merrienboer (Eds.), *Powerful learning environments: Unravelling basic components and dimensions* (89–107). Amsterdam: Pergamon.

European ODL Liaison Committee. (2004). *Distance learning and elearning in European policy and practice: The vision and the reality.* Retrieved September 1, 2005 http://www.odl-liaison.org/pages.php?PN=policy-paper_2004

Fabro, K. R., & Garrison, D. R. (1998). Computer conferencing and higher-order learning. *Indian Journal of Open Learning*, 7(1), 41–54.

Fink, L. D. (2003). *Creating significant learning experiences.* San Francisco: Jossey-Bass.

Friedman, T. L. (2005). *The world is flat: A brief history of the twenty-first century.* New York: Farrar, Straus and Giroux.

Frost, S., & Chopp, R. (2004). The university as global city: A new way of seeing today's academy. *Change*, 36(2), 44–51.

Garnham, C., & Kaleta, R. (2002). Introduction to hybrid courses. *Teaching with Technology Today*, 8(6). Online: http://www.uwsa.edu/ttt/ articles/garnham.htm

Garrison, D. R. (2003). Cognitive presence for effective asynchronous online learning: The role of reflective inquiry, self-direction and metacognition. In J. Bourne & J. C. Moore (Eds.), *Elements of quality online education: Practice and direction* (pp. 29–38). Volume 4 in the Sloan C Series, Needham, MA: The Sloan Consortium.

Garrison, R. (2004). Transformative leadership and e-learning. In K. Matheos and T. Carey (Eds.), *Advances and Challenges in eLearning at Canadian Research Universities* (pp. 46–54). CHERD Occasional Papers in Higher Education, 12, University of Manitoba.

Garrison, D. R. (2006a). Online collaboration principles. *Journal of Asynchronous Learning Networks*, 10(1), 25–34.

Garrison, D. R. (2006b). *Online community of inquiry review: Understanding social, cognitive and teaching presence.* Invited paper presented to the Sloan Consortium Asynchronous Learning Network Invitational Workshop, Baltimore, MD, August.

Garrison, D. R., & Anderson, T. (2003). *E-Learning in the 21st century: A framework for research and practice.* London: Routledge/Falmer.

Garrison, D. R., Anderson, T., & Archer, W. (2000). Critical inquiry in a text-based environment: Computer conferencing in higher education. *The Internet and Higher Education*, 2(2–3), 87–105.

Garrison, D. R., Anderson, T., & Archer, W. (2001). Critical thinking, cognitive presence and computer conferencing in distance education. *American Journal of Distance Education*, 15(1), 7–23.

Garrison, D. R., & Archer, W. (2000). *A transactional perspective on teaching-learning: A framework for adult and higher education*. Oxford, U.K.: Pergamon.

Garrison, D. R., & Archer, W. (2007). A community of inquiry framework for online learning. In M. Moore (Ed.), *Handbook of distance education*. New York: Erlbaum.

Garrison, D. R., & Cleveland-Innes, M. (2005). Facilitating cognitive presence in online learning: Interaction is not enough. *American Journal of Distance Education*, 19(3), 133–148.

Garrison, D. R., Cleveland-Innes, M., & Fung, T. (2004). Student role adjustment in online communities of inquiry: Model and instrument validation. *Journal of Asynchronous Learning Networks*, 8(2), 61–74. Retrieved August 13, 2005, from http://www.sloan-c.org/publications/jaln/v8n2/pdf/v8n2_garrison.pdf

Garrison, D. R., & Kanuka, H. (2004). Blended learning: Uncovering its transformative potential in higher education. *The Internet and Higher Education*, 7(2), 95–105.

Gladwell, M. (2002). *The tipping point: How little things can make a big difference*. New York: Little, Brown and Company.

Hartman, J. L., & Truman-Davis, B. (2001). Institutionalizing support for faculty use of technology at the University of Central Florida. In R. M. Epper & A. W. Bates (Eds.), *Teaching Faculty How to Use Technology: Best Practices from Leading Institutions* (pp. 39–58). Phoenix, Arizona: Oryx Press.

Hawkes, M., & Romiszowski, A. (2001). Examining the reflective outcomes of asynchronous computer-mediated communication on inservice teacher development. *Journal of Technology and Teacher Education*, 9(2), 285–308.

Heckman, R., & Annabi, H. (2005). A content analytic comparison of learning processes in online and face-to-face case study discussions. *Journal of Computer-Mediated Communication*, 10(2), article 7. http://jcmc.indiana.edu/vol10/issue2/heckman.html

Hewitt, J. (2005). Toward an understanding of how threads die in asynchronous computer conferences. *Journal of the Learning Sciences*, 14(4), 567–589.

Howe, N., & Strauss, W. (2000). *Millennials rising: The next great generation*. New York: Vintage Books.

Huber, M. T., and Hutchings, P. (2005). *The Advancement of Learning: Building the Teaching Commons*. San Francisco: Jossey-Bass.

Hutchings, P., & Shulman, L. E. (1999). The scholarship of teaching: New elaborations, new developments. *Change*, 31(5), 10–15.

Knowlton, D. S. (2003). Evaluating college students' efforts in asynchronous discussion: A systematic process. *The Quarterly Review of Distance Education*, 4(1), 31–41.

Kuh, G. D., Kinzie, J., Schuh, J. H., Whitt, E. J., and Associates. (2005). *Student success in college: Creating conditions that matter*. San Francisco: Jossey-Bass.

Kvavik, R. (2005). What do you want from online learning? Retrieved December 31, 2005 from http://learningarchitect.com/Newsletters/2005Dec/200512P01.htm

Kvavik, R. B., & Caruso, J. B. (2005). ECAR study of students and information technology, 2005: Convenience, connection, control, and learning. *Research Study from EDUCAUSE Centre for Applied Research*. Retrieved October 17, 2005, from http://www.educause.edu/ers0506/

LaPointe, D. K., & Gunawardena, C. N. (2004). Developing, testing, and refining a model to understand the relationship between peer interaction and learning outcomes in computer-mediated conferencing. *Distance Education*, 25(1), 83–106.

Levy, J. (2005). Envision the future of e-learning. *CIO Canada*, 13(2), 2. Retrieved Sept 2, 2005, from http://www.itworldcanada.com/a/CIO/1e9e4b1f-75e8-464b-a6fe-c4e05ec571d4.html

Lieberman, A. (1995). Practices that support teacher development. *Phi Delta Kappan*, 76(8), 591–596.

Lipman, M. (1991). *Thinking in education*. Cambridge: Cambridge University Press.

Luft, J. A. (1999). Rubrics: Design and use in science teacher education. *Journal of Science Teacher Education*, 10(2), 107–121.

Marquis, C. (2004). WebCT survey discovers a blend of online learning and classroom-based teaching is the most effective form of learning today. *WebCT.com*. Retrieved April 7, 2004, from http://www.webct.com/service/ViewContent?contentID=19295938

Marra, R. M., Moore, J. L., & Klimczak, A. K. (2004). Content analysis of online discussion forums: A comparative analysis of protocols. *Educational Technology Research and Development*, 52(2), 23–40.

Marton, F., & Saljo, R. (1976). On qualitative differences in learning: I. Outcome and process. *British Journal of Educational Psychology*, 46, 4–11.

McLuhan, M. (1964). *Understanding media: The extensions of man*. Toronto: McGraw-Hill.

Meyer, K. A. (2003). Face-to-face versus threaded discussions: The role of time and higher-order thinking. *Journal of Asynchronous Learning Networks*, 7(3), 55–65.

Meyer, K. A. (2006). When topics are controversial: Is it better to discuss them face-to-face or online? *Innovative Higher Education*, 31(3), 175–186. Published online. http://www.springerlink.com.ezproxy.lib.ucalgary.ca/content/3310553735m78u17/fulltext.pdf

Montgomery, K. (2002). Authentic tasks and rubrics: Going beyond traditional assessments in college teaching. *College Teaching*, 50(1), 34–39.

Murphy, E. (2004). Identifying and measuring ill-structured problem formulation and resolution in online asynchronous discussions. *Canadian Journal of Learning and Technology*, 30(1), 5–20.

Murray, J. P. (2002). Faculty development in SACS: Accredited community colleges. *Community College Review*, 29(4), 50–66.

Newman, D. R., Johnson, C., Cochrane, C. & Webb, B. (1996). An experiment in group learning technology: Evaluating critical thinking in face-to-face and computer-supported seminars. *Interpersonal Computing and Technology*, 4(1), 57–74. Retrieved March 30, 2005 from http://www.helsinki.fi/science/optek/1996/n1/newman.txt

Newman, D. R., Webb, B., & Cochrane, C. (1995). A content analysis method to measure critical thinking in face-to-face and computer supported group learning. *Interpersonal Computing and Technology*, 3(2), 56–77.

Newman, F., Couturier, L., & Scurry, J. (2004). *The future of higher education: Rhetoric, reality, and the risks of the market.* San Francisco: Jossey-Bass.

Novak, G. M., Patterson, E. T., Gavrin, A. D., and Christian, W. (1999). *Just-in-time teaching: Blending active learning with Web technology.* New Jersey: Prentice Hall Series in Educational Innovation.

Oliver, R., & Omari, A. (1999). Using online technologies to support problem based learning: Learners' responses and perceptions. *Australian Journal of Educational Technology*, 15(1), 58–79.

Paavola, S., Lipponen, L., & Hakkarainen, K. (2004). Models of innovative knowledge communities and three metaphors of learning. *Review of Educational Research*, 74(4), 557–576.

Palloff, R. M., & Pratt, K. (2005). *Collaborative online learning together in community.* San Francisco: Jossey-Bass.

Paulson, F. L., and Paulson, P. (1996). Assessing portfolios using the constructivist paradigm. In R. Fogarty (Ed.), *Student portfolios.* Palatine: IRI Skylight Training & Publishing.

Pawan, F., Paulus, T. M., Yalcin, S., & Chang, C. (2003). Online learning: Patterns of engagement and interaction among in-service teachers. *Language Learning & Technology*, 7(3), 119–140.

Perry, B., & Edwards, M. (2005). Exemplary online educators: Creating a community of inquiry. *Turkish Online Journal of Distance Education*, 6(2), Retrieved December, 8, 2005 from: http://tojde.anadolu.edu.tr/tojde18/articles/article6.htm

Preparing for the revolution: Information technology and the future of the research university. (2002). Washington, DC: National Academies Press.

Ramsden, P. (2003). *Learning to teach in higher education* (2nd ed.). London: Routledge.

Rice, R., Sorcinelli, M., & Austin, A. (2000). Heeding New Voices: Academic Careers for a New Generation. Working Paper Inquiry #7. Washington, DC: American Association for Higher Education.

Rocco, E. (1996). Cooperative efforts in electronic contexts: The relevance of prior face-to-face interactions. *Computational and Mathematical Organization Theory Workshop*, Washington, DC. Retrieved March 26, 2005 from http://64.233.167.104/search?q=cache:e-hG4SnB0YkJ:www.casos.ece.cmu.edu/pdf/1996.PDF+cooperative+efforts+and+elena+rocco&hl=en&start=8

Rovai, A. P. (2002). Sense of community, perceived cognitive learning, and persistence in asynchronous learning networks. *The Internet and Higher Education, 5*(4), 319–332.

Rovai, A. P., & Jordan, H. M. (2004). Blended learning and sense of community: A comparative analysis with traditional and fully online graduate courses. *International Review of Research in Open and Distance Learning, 5*(2), Retrieved December 14, 2005 from http://www.irrodl.org/content/v5.2/rovai-jordan.html

Sands, P. (2002). Inside outside, upside downside: Strategies for connecting online and face-to-face instruction in hybrid courses. *Teaching with Technology Today, 8*(6). Online: http://www.uwsa.edu/ttt/articles/sands2.htm

Schrire, S. (2004). Interaction and cognition in asynchronous computer conferencing. *Instructional Science: An International Journal of Learning and Cognition, 32*, 475–502.

Schweizer, K., Paechter, M., & Weidenmann, B. (2003). Blended learning as a strategy to improve collaboration task performance. *Journal of Educational Media, 28*(2–3). Retrieved July 12, 2006 from http://taylorandfrancis.metapress.com.ezproxy.lib.ucalgary.ca/media/d86tumrgurcj76qugt33/contributions/5/q/c/y/5qcy969bu9c702tf.pdf

Shea, P., Fredericksen, E., Pickett, A., & Pelz, W. (2003). A preliminary investigation of teaching presence in the SUNY learning network. *Quality Studies: Online Education Practice and Direction, 4*, 279–312.

Shea, P., Li, C. S., & Pickett, A. (2006). A comparative study of teaching presence and student sense of learning community in fully online and web-enhanced college courses. *The Internet and Higher Education, 9*(3), 175–190.

Shea, P., Pickett, A., & Pelz, W. (2003). A Follow-up Investigation of Teaching Presence in the SUNY Learning Network. *The Journal of Asynchronous Learning Networks, 7*(2), 61–80.

Shumar, W., & Renninger, K. A. (2002). Introduction: On conceptualizing community. In K. A. Renninger (Ed.), *Building virtual communities* (pp. 1–14). Port Chester, NY: Cambridge University Press.

Slavit, D., Sawyer, R., & Curley, J. (2003). Filling your PLATE: A professional development model for teaching with technology. *TechTrends*, 47(4), 35–38.

Smith, P. (2004). Curricular transformation: Why we need it and how to support it. *Change*, 36(1), 28–35.

Song, H-D, Koszalka, T. A., & Grabowski, B. L. (2005). Exploring instructional design factors prompting reflective thinking in young adolescents. *Canadian Journal of Learning and Technology*, 31(2), 49–68.

Swail, W. S. (2002). Higher education and the new demographics: Questions for policy. *Change Magazine*, 34(4), 15–23.

Swan, K., & Shih, L. F. (2005). On the nature and development of social presence in online course discussions. *Journal of Asynchronous Learning Networks*, 9, 115–136.

Tu, C., & McIsaac, M. (2002). The relationship of social presence and interaction in online classes. *The American Journal of Distance Education*, 16(3), 131–150.

Tuckman, B. W. & Jensen, M. C. (1977). Stages of small-group development revisited. *Group and Organization Studies*, 2, 419–427.

Twigg, C. A. (2003). Improving learning and reducing costs: New models for online learning. *Educause Review*, 38(5), 29–38.

University of Wisconsin-Milwaukee. (2002). Student reactions. *Hybrid Course Website*. Online: http://www.uwm.edu/Dept/LTC/student-reactions.html

Vaughan, N. D. (2004). *Investigating how a blended learning approach can support an inquiry process within a faculty learning community*. Doctoral dissertation, University of Calgary.

Vaughan, N., & Garrison, D. R. (2005). Creating cognitive presence in a blended faculty development community. *Internet and Higher Education*, 8, 1–12.

Vaughan, N., & Garrison, D. R. (2006a). How blended learning can support a faculty development community of inquiry. *Journal of Asynchronous Learning Networks*, 10(4), 139–152.

Vaughan, N., & Garrison, D. R. (2006b). A blended faculty community of inquiry: Linking leadership, course redesign and evaluation. *Canadian Journal of University Continuing Education*, 32(2), 67–92.

Voos, R. (2003). Blended learning: What is it and where might it take us? *Sloan-C View*, 2(1). Online: http://www.sloan-c.org/publications/view/v2n1/blended1.htm

Wegerif, R. (1998). The social dimension of asynchronous learning. *Journal of Asynchronous Learning Networks*, 2(1), 34–49.

Weigel, V. B. (2002). *Deep learning for a digital age: Technology's untapped potential to enrich higher education*. San Francisco: Jossey-Bass.

Windham, C. (2005). Father Google & mother IM: Confessions of a Net Gen learner. *EDUCAUSE Review*, 40(5), 42–58.

Index

A

Abrams, Z., 28, 36, 93
Adobe Presenter, 57, 66, 111, 115
Albrecht, B., 3–4
Allectra, 116
Anderson, T., 9
Andrade, H. G., 137
Annabi, H., 23, 45
Arabasz, P., 3
Arbaugh, J. B., 9, 25
Archer, W., 9, 14, 23
Assessment Reform Group, 140
Assessments: background knowledge probe, 136–137; guidelines for discussion and feedback, 100–103; increasing feedback opportunities with, 133; interview questions for faculty, 195; maintaining accountability and creditability with, 46–47; methods published in sample course outline for, 213–214; Minute Paper, 135–136; redesigning classes from student, 73; rubrics for student assignments, 119, 137–138, 139, 219–223; self-assessment and scoring guide for discussion forums, 130–131; strategies and tools for, 128–140; student portfolios in, 138, 140, 219–223; student survey questionnaire, 61, 189–193; techniques for classroom, 134–137. *See also* Surveys
Asynchronous communications, 85–86, 163
Atkins, D. E., 157
Ausubel, D. P., 113–114

B

Baker, M. B., 3
Barkley, E. F., 120
Barrett, H. C., 140
Bean, J. C., 120
Blackboard, 109, 110, 133
Blended faculty community of inquiry. *See* Faculty
Blended learning: about, x, 11; advantages of online and face-to-face learning in, 163–164; community of inquiry framework for, 8–10, 13; course design for, 5–7; creating campuswide support for, 63–66; facilitation strategies for, 112–128; innovations allowing, 145–146; integrating real and virtual communities, 26–29; interest in, 3–5;

Blended learning (*Cont.*)
introducing student to, 209–213; new approaches available for, 85–88; percentage of online courses offering, 49; policies required for adoption of, 164–171; preparing template for course outlines, 108, 205–206; redesign guide for, 55, 107, 177–179; role of direct instruction in, 44–45; sample course outline for, 207–218; student survey questionnaire on, 61, 189–193; teaching presence and classroom interaction in, 25; transforming higher education with, 143, 152–155; transition from passive to collaborative learning, 144–148. *See also* Redesign scenarios

Bonk, Curtis, 3, 64
Bourne, K., 4
Boyer Commission, The, 167
Brainstorming, 90–91, 92, 95
Brookfield, S. D., 123
Brown, Ruth, 20
Budgets for course redesign, 176
Burbules, N. C., 23

C

Cagle, A. B., 50–51
Calibrated Peer Review (CPR) tool, 81
Caruso, J. B., 86
CATs (classroom assessment techniques), 135
Celentin, P., 37
Chang, C., 15, 99, 132
Chemistry course, 77–79
Chickering, A. W., 108, 133

Chopp, R., 157
Christian, W., 116
Classrooms: assessment techniques for, 134–137; blended learning and innovations in, 147; developing community of inquiry within, 89–91; integrating with online learning, 6, 28, 30; Minute Paper assessments, 135–136; teaching presence and interaction in, 25; using online learning in, 6. *See also* Direct instruction; Face-to-face learning; Face-to-face sessions
Cleveland-Innes, M., 25, 28, 37
Cognitive presence, 21–24; categories and indicators of, 19; developing in blended learning environment, 35–38; encouraging progression of inquiry, 40–41; ensuring resolution of inquiry and metacognitive awareness, 43–44; facilitating, 94–96; guidelines designing, 90–92; illustrated, 18; orienting students to principle of, 110; practical inquiry model and, 21–22; sustaining in community of interest, 23
Cohesion. *See* Group cohesion
CoI. *See* Community of inquiry
Collaboration: on blended curriculum design, 56–58; challenges in assignments requiring, 91–92; collaborative constructivist process, 14; combining with reflection, 151–152; disciplined, 17; finding physical space for, 170; guidelines for using with direct instruction, 96–97, 98; as part of online learning process, 28–29; required

to create large enrollment course curricula, 76–77; supporting in direct instruction, 42; sustaining collaborative communication, 39–40, 47

Collaborative Learning Techniques (Barkley and associates), 120

Collins, J., 160

Communications: discussion forums between sessions as form of, 120, 123–124; establishing social presence encouraging, 33–35, 47; between face-to-face sessions, 120–126; freedom of in community of inquiry, 19–20; sustaining collaborative, 39–40; tools for before-session, 115–116; tools supporting synchronous, 58; using wikis for, 124; weblogs, 124–125; working with synchronous/asynchronous, 85–86, 163

Communications and writing course, 76–77

Community of inquiry (CoI): about, 9; academic discipline required in, 16–17; classroom climate for, 89–91; cognitive presence in, 18, 19, 21–24; developing blended faculty learning community, 51–53; elements of, 17–26; as framework for blended learning, 8–10, 13; illustrated, 18; inclusive nature of online communities, 24; integrating real and virtual communities in, 26–29; online and virtual communities, 27; openness in, 15–16; planning document for blended faculty community of inquiry, 181–187;

requirements for, 15; social presence in, 18, 19–21; strategies for creating, 106; teaching presence in, 18, 19, 24–26; triggering development of blended faculty, 53–56

Computer labs and support, 212–213

Concept reflection assignment, 133–134

Conrad, D., 25, 27

Constructivist learning theories, 13–14

Context in tipping point, 151–152

Courage in leadership, 160–161

Course outlines: creating, 107–108; posting as PowerPoint presentation, 111; preparing template for, 108, 205–206; providing for current course in redesign process, 175; sample, 207–218

Course redesign: for blended learning, 5–7; choosing tools based on, 105–106; considerations for inquiry during face-to-face sessions, 116–120; constructing course outline, 107–108; designing learning between F2F sessions, 120–126; facilitating, 60–61; funding for, 63; gaining support through faculty development programs, 165–166; gathering student feedback on, 61–62; guidelines for social and cognitive presence in, 88–92; incentives for, 170; increasing students accommodated with, 80; large enrollment class scenarios, 75–79; learning strategies before F2F sessions, 113–116; measuring

Course redesign (*Cont.*)
effect of, 169–170; as phase of blended faculty development, 59; preparation strategies for next F2F session, 126–128; preparing template for course outlines, 108, 205–206; project meetings for, 169–170; project proposal form for, 173–176; providing current course outlines for, 175; providing faculty "tip sheets" for, 64–65; questions directing selection of strategies and tools, 106–108; redesign guide for blended learning, 55, 107, 177–179; rethinking timing of classes, 81–82; small class course scenarios, 72–75; support course for, 168–171; sustainability plan for redesigned courses, 176; technology's role in, 52–53; triggering development of blended faculty, 53–56. *See also* Redesign scenarios

Cox, M. D., 51–52

CPR (Calibrated Peer Review) tool, 81

Cross, K. P., 120

Crouch, C. H., 117

Curley, J., 51

Curricula: collaborative development of large enrollment course, 76–77; developing blended curriculum collaboratively, 56–58; redesign plan for, 182

D

Data collection: gathering student feedback on course redesign, 61–62; measuring effect of course redesign project, 169–170; using student demographic data in course redesign, 107

Del.icio.us, 116

Designing community of inquiry: assessing intended outcomes, 46–47; challenges in, 33; creating social presence, 33–35, 47; developing cognitive presence, 35–38; direct instruction and, 41–45; facilitating discourse, 38–41; overview, 31–32; principles, 32, 47

Dewey, J., 14–15, 21, 26, 29–30

Digital classroom response systems, 78

Direct instruction: about, 41–42; ensuring resolution of inquiry and metacognitive awareness, 42–44; guidelines for, 96–100; strategies and tools for, 128–140; supporting collaborative learning, 42; teaching presence in design of blended learning experience, 44–45

Directing threaded discussions, 95–96, 97–98

Discipline in community of inquiry, 16–17

Discourse: assessing online, 101–103; defined, 38; encouraging progression of inquiry, 40–41; enhancing and sustaining social presence to facilitate, 38–41

Discussion as a Way of Teaching (Brookfield and Preskill), 123

Discussion forums, 129–132; difficulties arranging group discussions, 126; guidelines for directing threaded discussions,

95–96, 97–98; rubric to assess participation in, 138, 139; self-assessment and scoring guide for, 130–131; setting up expectations for, 129–130; student self-coding of contributions to, 131–132; using between sessions, 120, 123–124
Dixson, Marcia, 25
Document management system, 81
Drucker, Peter, 7
Duderstadt, J. J., 157

E

E-learning. *See* Online learning
"E-Learning the Millennial Generation", 64
Educational inquiry. *See* Community of inquiry; Inquiry; Practical inquiry model
Edwards, M., 25
Electronic portfolio system, 75. *See also* Portfolios
Elements of CoI framework, 17–26; cognitive presence, 18, 19, 21–24; illustrated, 18; overview of, 17–19; social presence, 18, 19–21; teaching presence, 18, 19, 24–26. *See also Specific elements*
Elluminate Live!, 58, 82, 109, 126
Engaging Ideas (Bean), 120
Entwistle, N., 103
Expectations: for discussion forums, 129–132; establishing course, 89–90, 109; publishing proposed outcomes in sample course outline, 208–209; setting assessment rubrics for assignments, 119, 137–138, 139; for student

attendance and participation, 214–215
Exploration phase of faculty development, 56–58

F

Face-to-face (F2F) learning: advantages in blended learning techniques, 163–164; deepening metacognitive awareness via, 98–99; designing environment for critical reflection via, 36–38; dualism between learning online and, 4–5, 48; establishing and sustaining social presence in, 34–35; face-to-face tutorials with TAs, 79; integrating classroom with online learning, 6, 28, 30; providing online learners with, 27; setting course expectations, 89–90, 109; understanding strengths of online and, 48. *See also* Face-to-face sessions
Face-to-face (F2F) sessions: between, 120–126; facilitating learning before, 113–116; preparing for next, 126–128; strategies to use during, 116–120; surveying results of, 117, 136
Facilitating blended learning, 112–128; before face-to-face sessions, 113–116; during face-to-face sessions, 116–120; between face-to-face sessions, 120–126; goals for, 112–113; phases for, 113; preparing for next face-to-face session, 126–128
Faculty: acquiring technological skills for blended learning, 183; adjusting course redesign based on

Faculty (*Cont.*)
student papers, 74–75; comments to interview questions, 201–204; creating campuswide support for blended, 63–66; developing large enrollment curricula collaboratively, 76–77; directing threaded discussions, 95–96, 97–98; dissatisfaction with learning experience, 10; engaging in scholarship of teaching and learning, 59–60; integrating and developing blended learning, 49–51; interview questions for, 61, 195; planning document for blended learning community of inquiry, 181–187; providing course redesign scenarios for, 71; schedule for blended community of inquiry, 183–187; "tip sheets" for course redesign, 64–65. *See also* Faculty development; Teachers

Faculty development: application/ resolution phase for, 59–63; developing blended faculty learning community, 51–53; exploration phase of, 56–58; gaining support for blended learning through, 165–166; integration phase of, 58–59; program outcomes for blended faculty community of inquiry, 57, 181–183, 187; scenario for, 166–171; triggering blended, 53–56; types of, 50–51

Faculty learning community (FLC), 51–53

Feedback: redesigning political science class from student, 73; strategies for classroom, 135–137; Web-based tools for, 133–134

Fink, L. D., 107

Frost, S., 157

Funding for course redesign, 63

Fung, T., 28

Furl, 116

Future trends: changes in learning, 143–144; tipping point for blended learning, 148–149; transition from passive to collaborative blended learning, 144–148

G

Gamson, Z. F., 108, 133

Garnham, C., 53

Garrison, D. R., 9, 14, 15, 23, 25, 28, 37, 98

Gavrin, A. D., 116

Gladwell, Malcolm, 149

Grabowski, B. L., 29

Graham, C. R., 64

Group cohesion: developing, 93; importance in community of inquiry, 38–39

Group discussions. *See* Discussion forums

Guidelines: assessing discussion and feedback, 100–103; design principles, 89–92; direct instruction, 96–100; facilitating social and cognitive presence, 92–96; new approaches for blended learning, 85–88

H

Hakkarainen, K., 15

Handbook for Blended Learning, The (Bonk and Graham), 64

Hawkes, M., 37

Heckman, R., 23, 45

Higher education: changes within institutions of, 144–145; changing leadership approaches to, 158–159; effect of communications technology on, 144; evolutionary transformation of, 152–153; ingredients in transformations of, 157; innovations in, 154–155; leadership and instructional approaches for contemporary, 162–164; policies required for adoption of blended learning approach, 164–171

Hornik, S., 50–51

Hounsell, J., 103

Huber, Mary, 51

Hutchings, Pat, 51, 59–60

I

Incentives for redesign, 170

Innovation: changes in learning institutions creating, 144–145; technology-inspired, 144

Inquiry: activities before face-to-face sessions supporting, 114; cognitive presence basic in, 21; Dewey's views of, 14–15; discipline required for, 16–17; encouraging progression of, 40–41; ensuring resolution of, 43–44; helping students achieve sense of resolution to course-related, 126–127; interaction and, 16; planning environment to support systematic, 35–38; strategies using practical, 112; undermining with excessive workloads, 91,

106. *See also* Practical inquiry model

Inquiry and blended learning (ITBL) course: about, 61–62; developing wiki resources, 65–66

Inquiry and Blended Learning Scholarship Dissemination Grant Program (University of Calgary), 63

Inquiry Through Blended Learning (ITBL) redesign support course, 168–171

Integrating: blended faculty community of inquiry, 49–51, 58–59; classroom with online learning, 6, 28, 30; real and virtual communities as community of inquiry, 26–29

Integration phase of faculty development, 58–59

Interaction: disciplined, 17; educational inquiry and, 16

Interpersonal skills of leaders, 160

Interview questions: faculty, 61, 195; faculty comments on, 201–204

J

Jordan, H. M., 26

Just-in-Time Teaching (JiTT), 116

K

Kaleta, R., 53

Kinzie, J., 119–120

Klimczak, A. K., 36

Knowlton, D. S., 102

Koszalka, T. A., 29

Kuh, G. D., 119–120

Kulhorst, M., 25

Kvavik, R. B., 86

L

Large enrollment class scenarios, 75–79

Leadership: changing approach to higher education, 158–159; characteristics required for, 159–162; instructional approaches and need for, 162–164; required by direct instruction, 96–97

Learning: changes in, 7–8; constructivist theories of, 13–14; contributing factors to higher-level, 29–30; deep and surface approaches to, 87–88; difficulty defining and measuring outcomes of, 23; dualism between face-to-face and online, 4–5; process of inquiry in, 15; students' responsibility for own, 42, 147. *See also* Face-to-face learning; Online learning

Learning experience: changes made from dissatisfaction in, 145; community of inquiry and, 14, 18–19; dissatisfaction with, 10, 146–147; engaging students in, 4; improving large enrollment course, 75–79; individual's struggle to make sense of, 30; interactive and reflective elements of, 16; potential to transform with blended learning, 27–29; practical inquiry model's representation of, 22; teaching presence and successful, 25

Learning Instructional Development Sub-committee (University of Calgary), 54

Learning management systems (LMS): creating online discussion forums within, 120, 123; demonstrating for students, 109–111; developing survey and quiz tools in, 116; increasing feedback and assessment opportunities with, 133; learning to use, 72, 73

Learning plans, 166–168

Lectures: complimenting with online tutorials, 79; engaging learners in, 4; redesigning scientific writing course, 80, 81; rethinking approach to learning beyond, 167

Levy, J., 7

Li, C. S., 35, 44

Library Connection, The, 109–110

Lieberman, A., 51

Lipman, M., 16

Lipponen, L., 15

Luft, J. A., 138

M

Major, C. H., 120

Marra, R. M., 36

Mazur, E., 117

McCune, V., 103

McLuhan, Marshall, 143

MERLOT (Multimedia Educational Repository for Learning Online Teaching), 117

Messenger rule in tipping point, 149–150

Metacognition: designing blended learning to develop, 43–44; encouraging, 98–100; guidelines for developing, 87–88; metacognitive processes, 25–26

Meyer, K. A., 36, 44–45, 93–94, 97

Minute Paper, 135–136

Montgomery, K., 138
Moore, J. L., 36
Murphy, L., 43–44

N

Net Geners, 86, 146, 147
Novak, G. M., 116
Nursing courses, 81–83

O

Online learning: advantages in blended learning techniques, 163–164; assessing online discourse, 101–103; coding student postings, 99; designing environment for critical reflection via, 36–38; dualism between face-to-face and, 4–5; effect of lack of social cues on, 20; establishing course expectations for, 89–90; expectation of teaching presence with, 25; guidelines for directing threaded discussions, 95–96, 97–98; impact on higher education, 144; juxtaposition of old pedagogy with new technology, 7–8; making traditional lectures more accessible with, 143–144; percentage offering blended learning, 49; pressure of workload in, 91, 106; providing orientation for, 211–212; reflective and collaborative process in, 28–29; support for cognitive presence in, 24; understanding strengths of face-to-face and, 48; using with face-to-face learning, 6; virtual communities, 27

Openness in community of inquiry, 15–16
Orientation for online learning, 211–212
Outcomes: for blended faculty community of inquiry, 57, 181–183, 187; published in sample course outline, 208–209

P

Paavola, S., 15
Paechter, M., 36
Palloff, R. M., 4
Patterson, E. T., 116
Paulson, F. L., 140
Paulson, P., 140
Paulus, T. M., 99, 132
Pawan, F., 99, 132
Peer Review Tool (PRT), 81
Pelz, W., 36
Perry, B., 25
Pew course redesign group, 149, 150
Philosophy course, 74–75
Pickett, A., 35, 44
Plenary sessions on blended learning, 63
Policies for blended learning, 165
Portfolios: sample assessment rubric for, 219–223; strategies for using, 138, 140; using electronic portfolio system, 75
Postings: placing PowerPoint presentations on Web, 78, 110, 111; self-coding, 99, 131–132
PowerPoint slides, 78, 110, 111
Practical inquiry model: cognitive presence and, 21–22; illustrated, 22; learning outcomes and, 23
Pratt, K., 4
Preskill, S., 123

Principles in blended learning design: creating social presence, 33–35; developing critical reflection and discourse, 35–38; encouraging progression of inquiry, 40–41; ensuring assessment congruent with intended outcomes, 46–47; ensuring resolution of inquiry and metacognitive awareness, 43–44; supporting students' collaborative learning, 42; sustaining community with collaborative communication, 39–40

Professional development. *See* Faculty development

Project meetings: course redesign project, 169–170; for integrating blended learning faculty development, 59

Project proposal form, 173–176

Project-based courses, 79–83

Proquest, 116

R

Ramsden, P., 46

Redesign guide for blended learning, 55, 107, 177–179

Redesign scenarios: about, 71; communications and writing course, 76–77; faculty development, 166–171; introductory chemistry course, 77–79; large enrollment course, 75–76; nursing course, 81–83; philosophy course, 74–75; political science class, 72–74; project-based courses, 79–80; scientific writing course, 80–81; small class course, 72

Reflection: combining with collaboration for context of blended learning, 151–152; concept reflection assignment, 133–134; as element of learning, 16; FLC engaged in process of, 52; focusing learning with, 133; in online learning, 28–29; planning for critical, 35–38

Reiff, A., 25

Relationships in community of inquiry, 20

Renninger, K. A., 27

Rocco, E., 92

Romiszowski, A., 37

Rovai, A. P., 26

Rubrics: assessing student assignments with, 119, 137–138, 139; defined, 137; sample portfolio assignment, 219–223

S

Sample materials: assessment rubric for portfolios, 219–223; blended learning course outline, 207–218; student survey questionnaire, 61, 189–193; student survey results, 61, 197–199

Sands, P., 53

Sawyer, R., 51

Scenarios. *See* Redesign scenarios

Schedule: blended faculty community of inquiry project, 183–187; published in sample course outline, 215–217

Scholarship of teaching and learning (SoTL), 59–60

Schrire, S., 15, 21, 32

Schuh, J. H., 119–120

Schweizer, K., 36

Scientific writing course, 80–81

Scoring guide for discussion forums, 130, 131

Seaman, J., 4

Seven Principles for Good Practice in Undergraduate Education (Chickering and Gamson), 108, 133

Shea, P., 35, 44

Shih, L. F., 38, 40

Shulman, L. E., 59–60

Shumar, W., 27

Slavit, D., 51

Smith, P., 172

Social bookmarking systems, 116

Social epidemics, 149

Social presence, 19–21; categories and indicators of, 19; creating, 33–35, 47; enhancing and sustaining to facilitate discourse, 38–41; establishing with online learning, 20–21; facilitating, 92–94; guidelines designing, 89–90; illustrated, 18; open communications and, 19–20; orienting students to principle of, 110; supporting students' collaborative learning, 42

Song, H-D., 29

SoTL (scholarship of teaching and learning), 59–60

Stickiness in tipping point, 150–151

Strategies and tools: direct instruction and assessment, 128–140; facilitating blended learning, 112–128; identifying needed, 105–106; including students in rationale for, 108–109; portfolios, 138, 140; questions directing selection of, 106–108. *See also* Facilitating blended learning

Student Success in College (Kuh and associates), 119–120

Student survey questionnaire, 61, 189–193

Student survey results, 61, 197–199

Students: assessment rubrics for assignments, 137–138, 139; attendance and participation expectations for, 214–215; benefits of community of inquiry for, 29; blended learning challenges for, 210–211; dissatisfaction with learning experience, 10, 146–147; engaging in process of inquiry, 14; expectation of strong teaching presence online, 25; freedom of expression in community of inquiry, 19–20; giving rationale for strategies and tools, 108–109; including in blended learning program evaluations, 58; increasing number accommodated with course redesign, 80; need for face-to-face and online interactions by, 86, 147, 153; negotiating expectations for learning, 89–90, 109; Net Gener learning and technology preferences, 86; orienting to learning management systems, 110; providing "tip sheets" on blended learning courses, 65; satisfaction with blended learning, 3–4; self-coding postings, 99, 131–132; showing resources and software applications, 109–111; supporting to assume

Students (*Cont.*)
responsibility for learning, 42,
147; using demographic data in
course redesign, 107
Surveys: course redesign feedback,
61–62; preparing for next F2F
sessions with, 127–128; results of
F2F sessions, 117, 136; results of
student survey questionnaire, 61,
197–199; student survey
questionnaire, 61, 189–193
Sustainability plan for redesigned
courses, 176
Swail, W. S., 7
Swan, K., 38, 40
Synchronous communications:
applications supporting
between-session communications,
126; asynchronous and, 85–86,
163; tools for, 58

T

TAs (teaching assistants), 77, 78
Teachers: acquiring face-to-face and
online skills and strategies, 182;
creating online community of
inquiry, 25; demonstrating
resources and software
applications, 109–111; e-mail
policies for, 215; incentives for
redesign, 170; interview questions
for, 61, 195; negotiating
expectations for learning, 89–90,
109; Net Gener preferences for
interaction with, 86; planting
seeds before face-to-face sessions,
113–116; using classroom
assessment techniques, 134–
137
Teaching assistants (TAs), 77, 78

Teaching, Learning Technology
Roundtable, 54
Teaching presence, 24–26; categories
and indicators of, 19; ensuring in
blended learning experience,
44–45; function of, 24–25;
guidelines for developing, 97–98;
illustrated, 18
Teaching. *See* Direct instruction;
Teaching presence
Technology: acquiring skills for
blended learning, 183; choosing
tools based on educational design,
105–106; computer labs and
support for blended learning
courses, 212–213; digital
classroom response system, 78;
educational innovations offered
by, 144; innovation requiring
more than, 145–146; Net Gener
preferences for blended, 86–87;
role in blended learning faculty
development, 52–53
Tip sheets for course redesign, 64–
65
Tipping point: blended learning's,
148–149; context in, 151–152;
messenger rule in, 149–150;
stickiness in, 150–151
Tipping Point, The (Gladwell), 149
Tools: for before-session
communications, 115–116;
questions directing selection of,
106–108; selected from course
redesign, 105–106; supporting
synchronous communications, 58.
See also Strategies and tools;
Web-based tools
Transforming higher education:
blended learning as means for,

27–29, 143, 152–155; ingredients in, 157; leadership needed for, 158–159; Web-based tools as way of, 8, 157, 158

Twigg, C. A., 64, 133, 149

U

University of Calgary, 53–54, 63, 109, 189–193

University of California Los Angeles, 81

University of Central Florida, 108, 165

University of Wisconsin-Milwaukee, 109

V

Van Houweling, D., 157

Vaughan, N. D., 34

Vision of future, 160

Voos, R., 53

W

Web sites: explaining resources and support found on, 109–111; providing support for course redesign on, 168; Web-based tools for feedback, 133–134

Web-based tools: choosing tools based on educational design, 105–106; developing ITBL wiki for, 65–66; feedback using, 133–134; posting class PowerPoint presentations on Web, 78, 110, 111; required by activities before face-to-face sessions, 114; transforming teaching and education with, 8, 157, 158; using classroom assessment techniques, 135

WebCT, 110, 133

Weblogs, 124–125

Wegerif, Rupert, 91

Whitt, E. J., 119–120

Wiki resources: developing, 65–66; example of online discussion summary, 124

Workloads and inquiry, 91, 106

Workshop on the Information Search Process for Research (WISPR), 110

Workshops: developing teaching strategies with blended learning, 64; disadvantages of skill-based, 50; initiating nursing course with, 82

Writing courses: communications and writing course, 76–77; scientific, 80–81

Y

Yalcin, S., 99, 132